Sickness—Why?
Healing—How?

Sickness—Why?
Healing—How?

By
Spiros Zodhiates, Th.D.

AMG
PUBLISHERS
Chattanooga, TN 37422

Sickness—Why? Healing—How?

ISBN 0-89957-491-2

Library of Congress Card Catalog Number:
99-72359

Printed in the United States of America

04 03 02 01 00 99 –B– 6 5 4 3 2 1

To my beloved physicians Dr. Don Snyder, Dr. Terry Orme, and Dr. Don Schlernitzauer who have been my friends and helpers.

The Lord can heal anyone at any time if it is His sovereign will to do so. When you are ill, we encourage you to pray to the Lord to be healed. If it is not His will to heal, then we know that someday we will be given a body that no disease whatsoever is going to affect (Rom. 8:23).

Contents

1

Where Does Sickness Come from, and Why Must I Face It?

The issue of sickness and healing is very divisive in the worldwide Christian community. Some say that God wants all His people to be healthy and that it is our lack of faith that prevents it. Others say that sickness is part of living in a fallen world and that healing happens when God determines it. Can this latter group be considered as lacking in faith—and thus missing healing? One group or the other misunderstands the Scriptures, and that is why we must thoroughly investigate the meanings of the Hebrew and Greek words which underlie the English texts of our Bibles.

We here at AMG International work with many sick people. We have hospitals in Greece, Guatemala, and India. We care for many leprosy patients with ulcerated hands whom we see praising God and praying. They fold their hands in prayer but may have no fingers on the stubs of their hands. Are we missing something? We would gladly pay the air fare to India for anyone who could heal them. Seeing the suffering of these lepers was the motivation for this study.

The first question we must ask is, What is man made of? Paul wrote, "And the very God of peace sanctify you wholly; and I pray God your whole spirit and soul and body be preserved blameless unto the coming of our Lord Jesus Christ" (1 Thess. 5:23).

The Spirit

Paul first mentions the spirit (Greek, *pneúma* [4151]; Hebrew, *rûah* [7307, OT]). Both words can be interpreted either as "spirit" or "breath." God is *pneúma,* spirit. This is what Jesus told the Samaritan woman in John 4:24. God cannot be touched or limited in what He can do.

Man is unique among God's creation, since a part of him is spirit, like God. And man's sickness traces back to the separation of his spirit from God's Spirit. Most do not see this when they think of sickness, but the core problem and the worst sickness that man suffers from is a problem with his spirit, not just his body.

Let us delve deeper into the nature of man. In Genesis we see that God created everything that man needed before He made him. Then, in Genesis 1:26 we read: "Let us make man in our image, after our likeness: and let them have dominion over the fish of the sea, and over the fowl of the air, and over the cattle, and over all the earth, and over every creeping thing that creeps upon the earth." God breathed into man *pneúma,* the breath of His life or spirit, which He did not do for anything else in the physical world. Thus man is unlike anything else in nature.

Man was also given a mind with the ability to plan ahead and to choose. Notice that Satan's words were, "You shall be as gods" (Gen. 3:5). He was implying that God's restriction about the tree of knowledge of good and evil was motivated by a jealous God who was protective of His position. Satan put pride in man's heart, and now man wants to be in control. This is the source of man's problems.

We know that Jesus had a human spirit. He showed this at His death when He said, "Father, into thy hands I commend my spirit" (Luke 23:46). That was His own human spirit. The raising of Jairus' daughter (Luke 8:55) shows that the little girl's spirit returned to her. The human personality is not complete unless the spirit is attached to the body and soul.

The Soul

All animals have souls. The soul comprehends both the spark of life and sentience. Without the soul, the flesh is dead, inanimate. That is the soul as the spark of life. But the soul also includes the capacity of the senses which allow all sentient beings to relate to the world around them.

Man, though he has the added dimension of spirit, is sometimes thought of only as dichotomous—body and soul, and sometimes as trichotomous—spirit, soul, and body. But as man certainly has each of the three elements, it is nonsense to argue over words. Whenever the spirit is not expressly mentioned, it is included with the soul. This understanding lumps the two immaterial parts of man's makeup into one, contrasting it with the material, or physical, body.

Like the spirit, the soul does not cease to exist after death (Rev. 6:9). God Himself, has a soul according to Scripture (Heb. 10:38). The Greek word for "soul" is *psuchḗ* (5590). Added to the Greek word *sṓma* (4983), "body," we get our English word "psychosomatic" which describes the interaction between our immaterial and material parts. In Scripture, both the spirit and the soul think, choose, and emote. Psychosomatic illnesses are caused primarily by the soul. The body suffers because of sickness in the soul—from which both may perish, if there is no healing.

Fallen Man

The work of Christ is called "reconciliation" (*katallagḗ* [2643]). It is that which bridges the separation and loss of fellowship and communication with God. The fall of man broke the link of fellowship between God and man, and this is the death God pronounced on mankind. Man's soul and body were separated from the spirit that God created in man. Man lost the desire to follow God and went and hid himself instead (Gen. 3:8). That is what Ezekiel 18:4, 24 means when it says that the soul who sins is the one who will die. Man's spirit does not control his soul. He therefore hides from God as Adam and Eve did. His spirit is dead to messages from God.

Both believers and unbelievers have spirits, but in the unbeliever they are sick unto death. Such a spirit can accept or reject God because fallen man can still hear His voice (Gen. 3:8), and God does not cease to call him until the ultimate separation of his spirit from his soul which occurs at death. After death, judgment is inevitable with no possibility of salvation (Heb. 9:27).

The redeemed man's spirit is able to praise God and fellowship with Him. Animals cannot praise, because their souls do not have accompanying spirits. How can you know whether your spirit is healthy or sick? Genesis 3:8 has the answer: "And they heard the voice of the Lord God walking in the garden in the cool of the day: *and Adam and his wife hid themselves.*" If you are running away and hiding from God, you are spiritually sick. Your spirit is still separated from God. This is the greatest sickness you have, and the greatest healing you need.

The Body

Sṓma is a living body. At death it is no longer *sṓma,* but rather *ptṓma* (4430), carcass. When a human dies, the soul/spirit is disengaged from the body. Ezekiel 18:24 teaches that the soul of the "sinner" (unbeliever) dies or goes to Hades (*Hádēs* [86]) if an unbeliever. Hades is the place of identifiable disembodied spirits, as the story of the rich man and Lazarus (Luke 16:19–31) shows. Both the rich man and Lazarus remained distinct personalities. One was redeemed, the other was not redeemed. (Since Jesus had not yet died as a sacrifice for man's sins, Lazarus' spirit could not yet ascend to heaven ; cf. Acts 1:10–11.)

Body of Sin

The original cause of all sickness was Adam's rebellion against God. Physical illness, along with anger, alcoholism, divorce, war—all of man's problems—came as a direct result of the spiritual sickness in man, and now all men are born spiritually sick. Paul called this condition "the body of sin" in Romans 6:6, and in so doing he said, "knowing this, . . ."

It is important to note that he used the Greek word *ginṓskontes* (1097), which means that we experientially learn that there is a constant struggle going on within us. Anyone who feels no spiritual struggle is either spiritually dead or totally deceived.

A person is also deceived if he thinks God owes him healing. What we deserve is sickness, because we all made the wrong spiritual choice in Adam. Paul says in Romans 5:12, ". . . by one man sin entered into the world, and death by sin. . . ." So everything that leads to death was brought into the world by man. We cannot blame God, because we brought it on ourselves through our disobedience in Adam. The consequence is "the body of sin."

In referring to "our old man" in Romans 6:6, Paul does not use the word "original" (*archaíos* [744]) man, since our original man was perfect. He uses *palaiós* (3820), old man—man as sin has made him to be—"the old man." In the case of believers, this old man "is crucified with Him [Jesus]." So Christ died for the believer "that the body of sin might be destroyed." He died so that our fallen nature would no longer be dominant over the spirit, if we are true believers. We see this clearly in the Greek verb *katargēthḗ* translated "destroyed." *Katargéō* (2673) is derived from *katá* (2596), an intensifying preposition; and *argéō* (691), which means rendered inactive or idle. It is foolish and dangerous to believe the old nature is gone or totally dead.

No Longer Slaves of Sin

Christ offered Himself for us "that henceforth we should not serve sin" (Rom. 6:6). Here, the word "serve" means to serve as a slave, for the Greek *douleúein* (1398) means to be enslaved. Before we became Christians our spirits were not controlled by God's Spirit, for they were in harmony with the sinfulness of our soul and body. We continued to work out sin in our bodies constantly. But after we became children of God through Christ Jesus, we were no longer servants or slaves to the body of sin.

However, we remain mortal and corruptible. This is the direct result of original sin, and many fail to see that what they think belongs to them now is really promised for a later time. At the present time, it is impossible for man to escape death. We do not yet have physical immortality. The Greek word for immortality is *athanasía* (110), from *a* (1), a negative meaning without, not, or no; and *thánatos* (2288), death or separation.

When our Lord returns we shall be changed. Our entire environment is dead or dying, and we are all part of it. We will all experience—unless Christ returns first—a separation (*thánatos*) when our body (*sṓma*) becomes a carcass (*ptṓma*). Our spirits will depart. Now we have mortal bodies. There is only one person (the Man Christ Jesus) who had incorruptibility and immortality. That is what Paul meant in 1 Timothy 6:16 when, referring to Christ, he wrote, "Who only has immortality." Jesus is the only one whose body did not decay in the grave.

Decay Remains

With that single exception, decay is going on continually, and sickness accompanies the process. We grow old because we are sinners by nature, part of the fallen human race which is under the judgment of God. This is true whether we are redeemed or not. Our body is *phthartós* (5349), corruptible. First Corinthians 15:53 tells us, "For this corruptible must put on incorruption, and this mortal must put on immortality." For the believer this *phthartós* body will be changed.

So we see that sickness can be spiritual; it can be soulish in origin. Our souls may sin through entertaining evil thoughts without involving our bodies, but sooner or later this does involve the body. We must understand that the body itself does not sin, because it is not capable of acting on its own. It is the soul, which acts in conjunction with the body, that activates the body to do things contrary to God's law.

Let us indeed desire and pray for healing, but not expect the perfection and total freedom from corruption which is not intended for us in this age.

2

Why God Permits Sickness

There are several Greek words that we shall examine in our study, but the main word is *asthéneia* (769), sickness. This really means weakness. It is made up of the privative *a* (1), meaning "without" or "not," and *sthénos* (n.f.), meaning "strength"; hence, without strength, weakness.

Now whenever we read the word "sickness" in the Old or New Testament, we immediately think of the physical part of man. However, man is a personality, and that personality is composed of spirit, soul, and body. When we read in the New Testament that a person was sick and then was healed by Christ, what did He heal? It is important to understand that He healed the total personality.

Today, psychology and psychiatry are built in part on the theory of psychosomatic diseases, that one's thoughts may cause a headache, for instance. A person's philosophy of life sometimes can cause depression, and deep depression will make it difficult for one's body to function well. So weakness or sickness of any part of the total personality—body, soul, or spirit—can cause diseases. These diseases in Greek are called *nósoi* (3554). In fact, modern medicine uses the term "nosology" which is the study of particular diseases.

Diseases can be classified as diseases of the body, diseases of the mind, and diseases of the spirit or soul. Spiritual diseases are those having to do with the relationship between a man and his Creator. An atheist, for instance, is a sick person, sick in his spirit. His spirit does not function as God intended.

The fact is that when the Lord Jesus died on the cross, He did not annihilate corruption within our present bodies. Sickness (*asthéneia*) may be most noticeable in our bodies, but it may also be present, and perhaps commenced, in our emotional or spiritual parts.

Are Physicians and Medicine Necessary?

There are two Greek words for healers: *iatrós* (2395), healer, from the verb *iáomai* (2390), to heal, referring specifically to bodily healing; and *therápōn* (2324), from the verb *therapeúō* (2323), from which we get "therapy" and "therapeutic." But a *therápōn* is actually more than an *iatrós* (physician) because the *therápōn* takes care of more than the body. He has a concern for the total personality—something we have largely lost in this present age of specialization.

What should we do when we are sick? Should we pray, or should we take a pill, or see a doctor? Should we refuse to see a doctor because that would be "unspiritual"? Certainly prayer is cheaper than going to a doctor! But because prayer costs nothing, while medical treatment may cost a great deal, is that the way to decide? Does God give us license to eat whatever we want and live however we want, if only we remember to ask Him to keep us healthy? What is the right approach to healing and healthy living for a Christian? Where is the balance?

We can gain some light on this subject by asking the same type of questions about food. Could we not simply ask God to supply the food we and our families require? It would be a lot easier and cheaper than working to earn our daily bread. And we know that God could provide for our needs in this way if He wished to do so, for did He not provide manna from heaven for forty years for the multitude of Israelites?

But we are in very different circumstances than were the Hebrews during their long trek from Egypt to the Promised Land. God *could* feed us, and He *could* heal our every disease, but He sovereignly does what He knows is best, meanwhile expecting us to recognize and respect His laws that He has instituted.

Again, think of the virgin birth of our Lord. His human body was supernaturally conceived within Mary's womb, but God did not set aside His natural law of gestation. Jesus' body was in Mary's womb nine full months, though God could have brought about her pregnancy one day and the birth of her baby the next. Just so, there are laws today that govern our physical bodies, our minds, our psyches, our souls, our spirits; and one of the greatest things that we can do as followers of God is to discover and use those laws, though not leaving aside prayer or thinking that God cannot change laws whenever He chooses.

So it is not a question of whether to pray or medicate, but to do both. And in what order? Let us look to James for light: "Is any sick among you? Let him call for the elders of the church; and let them pray over him, anointing him with oil in the name of the Lord. . . ." (James 5:14). First they were to anoint the sick person; then they were to pray. "Anointing" in Greek is *aleípsantes* (218), which really means having rubbed with ointment. They were first to apply the healing ointment, and then pray.

In "the prayer of faith" in verse 15, *euchḗ* (2171), translated as "prayer," means a vow; thus coupled here with faith, it is a vow of faith. We do that which is necessary, that which we know to do, but not knowing the sufficiency or efficacy of that which we have done, we vow that we are going to abide in faith—and faith means trusting God to do His part.

What Was the Jewish View of Sickness?

Remembering that James' instruction was given in the then-current Jewish culture, it will be helpful to examine what the widely-held attitude toward physical sickness was at that time. A most interesting story recounted in 1 Kings 17 gives us insight: Elijah, hiding from the wrath of the king, first hid by the brook Cherith, and after it dried up God sent him to a widow in Zarephath. There, after an act of obedience and faith on her part, Elijah remained in her household. But later her son became gravely ill and then died. Now notice this grieving mother's attitude, as expressed in her remonstrance to the prophet: "And she said unto Elijah, What have I to do with you, O you man of God? are you come unto me to call my sin to remembrance, and to slay my son?" (v. 18). In other words, she believed her past sins were responsible for her son's death.

If Elijah had been privy to the whole mind of God, he might have said, "Now wait a minute. This is not the way it works." But instead, his subsequent words reveal that he shared her misconception: "O Lord my God, have you also brought evil upon the widow with whom I sojourn, by slaying her son?" (v. 20). So we see that one of the greatest prophets of the Old Testament also embraced the belief that unconfessed sin is the actual cause of suffering and death in an individual's life.

This ancient error, compounded with more false belief, surfaced again in the episode of the blind beggar (John 9:1–2): "And as Jesus passed by, He saw a man which was blind from his birth. And His disciples asked Him, saying, Master, who did sin, this man, or his parents, that he was born blind?" They knew the man had been blind from birth, yet they asked if it was his sin or his parents' which was responsible for his blindness. How could he possibly be responsible, if as an innocent baby he was born blind?

Some early Jewish theologians taught that it was possible for unborn children to sin while still in the womb. They based this on Genesis 25:22 in which Esau and Jacob are reported to have struggled in Rebekah's womb. An alternative belief that souls exist before they are embodied, and could sin in that preexistent state, was also held by a few of the ancient scribes and was, therefore, part of the religious background.

What Was Jesus' View?

Jesus spoke against all such errors: "Neither has this man sinned, nor his parents: but that the works of God should be made manifest in him" (John 9:3). None of them was responsible for the man's blindness. Let us never lose sight of the basic fact, however, that all illness and all suffering are the result of the original disobedience of Adam and Eve.

An unbeliever has no relationship with God; he has no use for God. So when he is sick all he can do in his illness is suffer and be miserable. But the believer, although subject to the same ills of the flesh as the unbeliever, is in fellowship with God. He knows who his Healer is, and he says, Lord, what are You trying to teach me? Sickness never occurs in a vacuum. There is always a purpose in it, and that is what the Lord Jesus implies.

Now I want to bring out a word here in John 9:2–3 that is used in the original Greek text; it is *hína* (2443), "that": "Master who did sin, this man, or his parents, that he was born blind?" *Hína* can either denote result or purpose. In the disciples' question it denotes result, but in Jesus' response it denotes purpose: "Neither hath this man sinned, nor his parents: but that the works of God should be made manifest in him." That is purpose. In other words, we must never arrive at the conclusion that God, in order to show how great He is, makes a person blind. No, He takes a person who is the product of original sin and demonstrates His power in and through that person.

God uses sickness to reveal His glory. And the most important thing He can do, as far as Christians are concerned, is not primarily to heal them, but to help them develop an attitude of faith and grace in sickness. Think of stories you have heard of Christians suffering from cancer and other dreadful diseases and how wonderfully they have praised God.

Does Satan Cause Sickness?

Satan certainly plays a role in illness and has from the very beginning since he enticed Eve to taste the forbidden fruit in the Garden of Eden. Satan is, as the New Testament tells us, the chief of the principalities of the air. He is all around, but we must not give him more credit than he is due. We should understand that there is nothing that Satan can do without God's permission—whether in regard to nations or individuals.

Luke 13:10–16 tells the story of Jesus healing a crippled woman who suffered for eighteen years. She could not stand upright; she was bowed down. This woman had "a spirit of infirmity"—in the Greek, *asthéneia,* sickness or weakness, as we saw earlier. After Jesus laid His hands on her and healed her, He was accosted by the leader of the synagogue for healing on the Sabbath. The Lord replied in part: "And ought not this woman . . . whom Satan hath bound. . . ?" He understood her illness as being caused by Satan's action. It was caused in this woman by an evil spirit within her. She was a "daughter of Abraham," a Hebrew; however, she could not have contracted her disease while a follower of Jesus, since she had suffered from it for eighteen years.

Could, then, a believer today be inwardly bound by an evil spirit, or spirit of infirmity? We answer, "No," based on 2 Corinthians 12:7. Recall that Paul had been granted an experience so exalting that even after fourteen years he still could not put it into words. Then Paul says that God, in order to keep him from becoming puffed up, sent him a "thorn in the flesh, the messenger of Satan to *buffet* him." A buffet is a heavy blow. We need not concern ourselves here with the nature of that satanic attack. The point is that it came from without, not within. The same word "buffet" is used in Matthew 26:67 to describe the blows the Jewish leaders rained upon Christ Jesus before they handed Him over to the Romans. Satan was not inside Christ or Paul, but was attacking them from the outside.

For Jesus, this attack came as a prelude to the cross, and then glory. For Paul, it was the prelude to the glorious lesson that "when I am weak, then am I strong," because God's strength is made perfect in our weakness (2 Cor. 12:10).

3

The Apostles' Versus Today's Healing Ministry

We know that the consequences of Adam and Eve's sin, recorded in Genesis 3, were sickness and death upon all humanity. But does becoming a Christian then exempt us from sickness and death?

"Like Passions"

Some people believe that Christ died not only for our sin, but also for our infirmities (*astheneías* [769]). Based on this, they say that believers are spared from illnesses. Remember that God said that Adam and Eve would die if they disobeyed His command, and after they did disobey, they both hid themselves from God. That was the immediate death God spoke about. It was the separation of man's spirit from God's Spirit. Salvation reunites those spirits when God comes within that person.

However, each individual believer still has a body, and that body is still corruptible. It is the same aching body he had as a nonbeliever. We know this because when the people of Lystra (Acts 14:15) tried to worship Barnabas and Paul, they were stopped by the apostles who told the throng that they were not gods, but "men of like passions." They were *hómoioi* (3668), the same. They had the same weaknesses of body. Their spirits were reunited to God, but their bodies and souls were still corruptible.

The same thing is said of Elijah (James 5:17). He, too, had "like passions." He was an *ánthrōpos* (444), a man. He performed great miracles (1 Kgs. 17:1, 20–23, etc.), but he was only a man and grew weary and hungry (1 Kgs. 19:1–8), as does all mankind. Elijah was spared from death, not because he was a miracle worker, but as a type of Christ, foreshadowing His ascension.

Limited to the Twelve

In order to properly understand Scripture we must first observe, then interpret, and thirdly apply. This would prevent much false doctrine. Failure to understand that certain instructions and commands given by the Lord Jesus were restricted to just the Twelve for a specific purpose will lead to a wrong application.

There are many today making claims to be healers. They do this by taking upon themselves specific commands and promises given to the Twelve. Their claim is that we can do what they did and even as Christ did, forgetting that we are neither Christ nor apostles. In Matthew 10:1 Jesus gave the Twelve specific authority against evil spirits. The verbs "to *cast them out,* and to *heal* all manner of sickness and all manner of disease" is in the present infinitive (*ekbállein* [1544] and *therapeúein* [2323]) which means when opportunity presented itself. Do we have the same authority? No, that group was the Twelve. In verse 2 through 4 they are specifically named. This is confirmed in Matthew 11:1 where it says, "when Jesus had made an end of commanding His twelve disciples. . . ." These are limited commands to a limited group.

When we examine Luke 6:13–17, three groups of people are clearly pointed out. The first group is the Twelve whom Jesus called "apostles" and whose names are listed in verses 14 to 16. The second group (v. 17) is called "His disciples." These are clearly differentiated from the Twelve by the words *óchlos* (3793) *mathētṓn* (3101), an unorganized group of disciples. The third group (v. 17) is "a great multitude of people." These are the *plḗthos* (4128), the many people.

So, when a verse says, "His twelve disciples," it is very specific. This does not allow us to always apply what they were told to ourselves. If it did apply to us, we should adhere to what and how they worked. We would be restricted to the same rules as they were and, I'm sure, would find them quite chafing.

Philip, in Acts 8:4–8, came to Samaria. The Lord had commanded the apostles not to enter any city of the Samaritans (Matt. 10:5). This Philip, however, was not Philip the apostle (Matt. 10:3), but Philip the evangelist who was appointed as a deacon to serve at tables (Acts 6:5; 21:8). In Samaria, the unorganized multitudes were seeing the signs which he did (Acts 8:6). He also cast out unclean spirits (v. 7) and many paralyzed and lame people were healed.

Before Philip came to Samaria, there was a magician called Simon who "bewitched the people of Samaria giving out that himself was some great one" (v. 9). It is clear that neither Simon's magic tricks nor Philip's signs that he did were of the caliber of apostolic exorcisms, healings, and cleansings. The activities of Philip did not always generate saving faith in Christ since even Simon the magician was baptized as he watched and "wondered" (Acts 8:13) about the miracles and signs Philip performed. When two apostles, Peter and John, were sent from Jerusalem to Samaria to investigate the phenomenon, they found that the Holy Spirit had not yet come upon them. Philip could not be classified as an apostle, like the Twelve.

Specific Power

Sometimes the Twelve, like religious leaders today, wanted power when they should not have it. James and John (two of the Twelve), when rejected at a Samaritan village, wanted to bring down fire on its inhabitants as Elijah did (Luke 9:54). Remember that Jesus' intent was to go to Jerusalem: "He steadfastly set His face to go to Jerusalem" (v. 51). The Twelve, however, wanted to hurry things up. They took an opportunity where and when they were not authorized. Then note how their attitude changed from ministry to anger! Jesus did not give them the power which they sought. He would not give any individual human being the right to exercise such judgment. Jesus limited their power.

We should also note in Matthew 28:18–20, the so-called "Great Commission," that Jesus holds the authority. He had not relinquished that authority to the Twelve or to us. Notice also that He did not tell His disciples that they would have the same power as the Twelve.

In 2 Corinthians 11:5, the apostle Paul dealt with the "super-apostle" problem. These *hupér* (5228) *lían* (3029, "super" [see 5228, II, B]) men were taking on themselves the claim of permanent individual power without recognizing that the Twelve were unique.

Just because Elijah or Paul or the Twelve acted in certain circumstances does not mean that we may. Christ keeps the authority. The Twelve were given in Matthew 10 (cf. Mark 6:7ff.; Luke 9:1ff.) specific power for specific witness under specific historical situations.

There are some frightening ideas present in some thinking that they are "apostles." Can they rewrite Scripture? Can they add to or subtract from it? This cannot be so. They do not have the authority to do so (Rev. 22:18–19).

Specific Witness

Besides being given unique power, the Twelve were given a unique mission field. They were, according to Matthew 10:6, to go only to "the lost sheep of the house of Israel" and forbidden to go to the Gentiles or even to the Samaritans (v. 5).

When you preach to the Jews, Jesus told them, heal all kinds of weaknesses you see among them. We are simply not observing the restrictions in this passage if we assume the same claim to power and authority. If someone claims the same power and authority of the apostles, it comes from a failure to observe and interpret, resulting in a faulty application, and it could be a mere ego trip.

A Specific Time and Circumstance

We must also observe that Jesus' commands were for *that* particular time. Otherwise, the "Great Commission" of Matthew 28:18–19 is violated. In reality, though, it is not so much the "Great Commission" as it is the "Great Affirmation." It is not so much "Go ye therefore," but " having gone," and then follows the aorist imperative: *mathēteúsate* (3100), make disciples, in other words, "Having gone, you will make disciples." This is really a wonderful promise to Jesus' followers that the gospel message will bring results. It will be effective.

To whom is this promise given? To all Christ's disciples in all nations. It was never Jesus' intent to permanently keep the Gentiles out, but there was a particular job at a particular time that needed to be done.

Note also that in Acts 8 we have the record of Peter and John, two of the Twelve, going to Samaria (v. 14). These two obviously did not raise the issue of whether by going to Samaria they were violating Jesus' earlier order in Matthew 10:5. That order no longer applied to them.

We have seen this same principle at work in the Lord supplying manna while His people were in their wilderness wanderings, but cutting off that supply once they entered the Promised Land. God acts according to the circumstances He permits and brings into His people's lives.

Today's Application

What general application to our time can we draw from Jesus' words to the Twelve in Matthew 10?

First, it is imperative (present imperative) that we continually witness (v. 7). That is the same emphasis as the Great Commission (Matt. 28:18–19). When we find someone who is sick, what are we to do? We are to "heal the sick" (v. 8). The Greek word translated "heal" is not *iatreúō* (n.f.), or *iáomai* (2390), which means "heal," but it is *therapeúō,* to minister. We are to tenderly minister to people's needs. We are to minister to their total personality—spirit, soul, and body. We are to keep preaching and ministering. Paul gives the same advice to Timothy to "preach the word" (2 Tim. 4:2), and then *epístēthi* (2186), get close to the people in determining their individual needs and meeting them.

Jesus is stressing that, like the good Samaritan who saw a need and met it, we are to do the same. As we preach, we come across needy people. That is why AMG has a leprosy work in India and child-care centers throughout the world. We preach the word, and as we come across great needs, we attempt to minister to them.

Grace Is Not for Sale

Now, one of the restrictions Jesus gave in Matthew 10 is financially related. This restriction is certainly not applied by many faith healers today! The Twelve were to travel lightly and take no money (vv. 9–10). The application is that we are not to make a profit out of our ministry. Grace is not for sale.

Go back to Acts 8:18–24 and note how Simon wanted the power to work miracles. Many today want it, too. Peter and John strongly rebuked Simon (vv. 20–23) because the power of God was not for sale. Yet today "healers" need so much money!

Jesus said, "Freely you have received, freely give" (Matt. 10:8). The word "freely" could be misunderstood as "abundantly," but it should not be. It is *dōreán* (1432), without charge. We are not to charge people for giving them what we have received without cost. The free gift of the Holy Spirit is called *chárisma* (5486). The gifts of God's grace are received freely, so we are to make no charge in exercising them.

Another application for us is that we are to do the work of ministry and God will provide. Jesus reminded His disciples of this in Luke 22:35: "When I sent you without purse, and scrip, and shoes, lacked you anything? And they said, Nothing." Where God guides, God provides. The people who benefit from our ministry will help provide our needs (Matt. 10:10), and God will never let us down. Paul wrote, "Even so has the Lord ordained that they which preach the gospel should live of the gospel" (1 Cor. 9:14). There is a verb in the Greek New Testament which is translated "corrupt" used with reference to the Word of God. It is the verb *kapēleúō* (2585). It means to dilute or adulterate something and then to sell it cheaply. We are not permitted to misrepresent the gospel and then charge for it.

The misapplication of Matthew 10:8 by the "healing" ministries around us today is an example of how a verse can be taken out of its context to create false doctrine. Not observing closely and interpreting carefully is a dangerous way to handle the Scriptures.

4

Jesus Was Not Sick, Why Us?

One of the characteristics of false teachers described in detail in 2 Peter 2:10–19 is "they understand not" (v. 12). What is it that today's faith healers do not understand?

"They Understand Not" Apostolic Weakness

When we examine the Scriptures, we find no evidence to indicate that the original twelve disciples were ever sick, but nevertheless they all died. They were all subject to the corruptibility of their bodies, and just because they became believers, they were not exempted from sickness or death. Death is the ultimate form of sickness.

We have a specific example of apostolic illness in the life of Paul. There is no question that Paul was a genuine apostle and he defends this in 1 Corinthians 9:1. Yet in 2 Corinthians 12:7 we find Paul describing his "thorn in the flesh," his sickness. (This is discussed by

Paul in the context of his experience of being lifted up to the third heaven [vv. 1–6]. Consider also that his experience exceeds the experiences of Peter, James, and John on the Mount of Transfiguration [Matt. 17:1ff., cf. Mark 9:2ff.; Luke 9:28ff.]. They saw Moses and Elijah come down, but Paul experienced heaven itself.)

Paul says in 2 Corinthians 12:5 that ". . . of myself I will not glory, but in my infirmities." This is the Greek word *astheneías* (769), my weaknesses or sicknesses. Now, if the faith healer's interpretation of Matthew 8:17 is correct, and Jesus died for our sicknesses, why did He not take Paul's? Paul clearly rejoiced in them, and he knew they were sent to keep him humble (2 Cor. 12:7). Most theologians conjecture that this was an eye problem. So another conclusion we can draw is that not all infirmities are given as punishment (John 9:3). The faith healer does not understand and think through the conclusion of apostolic death or illness.

"They Understand Not" God's Wisdom

Faith healers also fail to understand the wise purpose of God in using infirmities for His glory. Paul clearly says in 2 Corinthians 12:7 that God had a purpose behind his infirmity. Satan may be allowed to hit and slap us about, but we must see that behind Satan's hand is the sovereign hand of God.

Paul may also have had a problem with malaria! In Acts 13:13 it is recorded that "Paul and his company loosed from Paphos," and "they came to Perga" by boat. Perga is a seacoast town with mosquito-infested marshes, and possibly here at Perga Paul may have contracted malaria. Paul was human and needed help, but this is where John Mark abandoned him. Paul then went to Antioch in Pisidia (v. 14) which was in Galatia, from sea level to around 3000 feet elevation. Could it be to get away from those marsh mosquitoes?

God did not eliminate the physical handicaps the great apostle had to endure. Did his problems limit the gospel? No. Paul, in his weakness, preached one of the greatest sermons in Antioch he had ever delivered (Acts 13:16ff.). The whole city came out to see and hear him. Today's faith healers do not understand that what is man's extremity is God's opportunity.

"They Understand Not" Jesus' Uniqueness

Faith healers do not closely observe the Scriptures. They say that since Jesus did something, we should, too. They can see His similarity to us, but they do not notice the differences.

We know that Jesus was subject to the laws of natural growth. He was supernaturally conceived but born in the natural way. He stayed in Mary's womb for nine months, and she nursed her infant. We also know that He got tired. John 4 records that Jesus became weary. He needed to refresh Himself. This shows us that we should take care of ourselves and respect the laws of nature. For example, we cannot deduce that since the children of Israel were fed in the desert or that since Jesus fed the multitudes, we can expect God to feed us today or that we should be able to duplicate His actions.

There are some very significant differences between Jesus and His believers. Jesus took upon Himself a human nature but not a sinful nature. Nowhere do we read that He was ever sick, had a headache, or any such thing. When He took on a body, it was without sin. He did not inherit our sin, and therefore did not inherit our sickness either. Hebrews 4:15 says that Jesus Christ our High Priest is not so indifferent to us that He "cannot be touched with the feeling of our infirmities." He suffers with us because He sees how sin mars our lives. The word "infirmities" is *astheneías.* He does not remove them; He suffers with us. He was "tempted [*pepeirasménon* {3985}] like as we are, yet without sin." He experienced temptation but did not and could not sin (1 John 3:5) because He did not have a sinful nature. Jesus willingly suffered as a consequence of our sin, but not for His own, since He had none (2 Cor. 5:21).

Another important difference between Jesus and believers is that Jesus' body was called "sacred," whereas ours are called "holy." In Acts 2:27 it says, "neither wilt Thou suffer Thine Holy One to see corruption." The word for "Holy One" is *hósios* (3741). It refers to the nature of being, that He was consecrated. Jesus' body was sacred, a body prepared for sacrifice, whereas the Christian's body is "holy" (*hágios* [40]), which refers to character. Jesus did not die of sickness but gave up His life. Man did not take it from Him.

Because Jesus did not have a sinful human nature and had a sacred body, it was not corruptible like ours. Acts 2:27 further says He would not "see corruption," for His body was incorruptible (*áphthartos* [862]). We have now a corruptible (*phthartós* [5349]) body which must be changed to an incorruptible (*áphthartos*) one.

Today's faith healers are too simplistic. We are not what Jesus was, so how can we claim for ourselves what does not belong to us? Faith healers do not understand the uniqueness of Jesus.

But What About John 14:12?

Faith healers today stand largely upon John 14:12: "Verily, verily, I say unto you, He that believes on Me, the works that I do shall he do also; and greater works than these shall he do; because I go unto My Father." Truly, this was a stupendous promise, and since it was a promise of our Lord, it could not fail to be fulfilled. But we must ask first, what is the nature of the works our Lord performed; and secondly, was this promise fulfilled by His apostles?

We have already seen—and will further elaborate in due course—that healing was peripheral to Jesus' purpose in coming to planet earth. His central purpose was to point man back to God and to become, to as many as would respond, their Redeemer as the sacrificial Lamb. Everything our Savior did on earth contributed to this central purpose, including healing.

If healing had been central to our Lord's mission, as some insist, there are great inconsistencies in His actions. Why, if He came primarily to heal, did He not heal all the "great multitude of impotent folk, of blind, halt, withered, waiting for the moving of the water" beside the pool of Bethesda in Jerusalem (John 5:3)? He healed only one of that great throng! Surely, He lost a wonderful opportunity to do good—if healing was His primary mission.

How did healings contribute to fulfilling Jesus' objective? They testified that He was indeed the Messiah who the Scriptures had foretold would appear. They were signs that attested to His divinity, signs that forced even the unwilling to acknowledge that One greater than man was among them. While not forgetting that our Lord was the soul of compassion, and that He felt deeply the hurts and miseries of all mankind, it must be insisted that His acts of healing always contributed to establishing Himself as the Son of God—both in first-century eyes and down to present-day eyes.

Again, as Peter and John continued our Lord's ministry, why did they invoke the power of God to heal just one lame beggar outside the temple (Acts 3:2–8)? Was he the only beggar they could have healed? Absurd thought! No, he was singled out at the Holy Spirit's bidding to be healed as a sign of their apostleship.

The direct application of "greater works" is to "the words that I speak unto you" found in John 14:10. It was His teaching ministry that was at the heart of His promise, and we maintain that it was of this that He spoke.

"Greater works than these shall he do." Jesus spoke to hundreds, and on some occasions to thousands. But we read in Acts 2:41 that about 3,000 were added to the body of Christ in one day upon hearing Peter's preaching. Acts 13:49 tells us "the word of the Lord was published throughout all the region." The book of Acts is full of the mighty preaching and revival that God brought about through them. Not only the Jews heard the gospel, but the Gentiles also. Today, thanks to our media of mass communication, we can transmit His message to hundreds of thousands, and even to millions, simultaneously.

"Greater works . . . shall he do." Jesus in the flesh was one Person—divine, but singular. But with the coming of the Holy Spirit, Jesus multiplied Himself through His followers. He speaks today through thousands of lips, as men filled with the Holy Spirit give forth the Master's message.

If one insists that a healing ministry today is legitimately based on John 14:12, let us note that the signs Jesus did included turning water into wine, raising the dead, walking on the water, calming the storm, and feeding thousands with a few loaves of bread and fish. These actions are not reproduced today.

"They Understand Not" God's Timing

The Bible clearly teaches that all the corruption around us is the result of original sin. Paul says in Romans 8:21, ". . . the creature itself also shall be delivered from the bondage of corruption." The word "creature" would be better understood as "creation" (*ktísis* [2937]). All of our world is pictured as restored in Revelation 21:1 where all things are new. *Kainós* (2537) means qualitatively new. Corruptibility will be replaced by a radically new, incorruptible world.

Notice also that man "*shall* be delivered" That is a future tense. We are not now delivered from corruptibility. We are going to have to endure our corruptible bodies and wait for God's timing. It is His determination. He is sovereign, and we cannot push His timetable.

Also note that creation will be delivered. The word is *eleutherōthḗsetai* (1659), will be "delivered free" or "loosed." Paul says that the creation is in a kind of slavery but will be freed to "the glorious liberty of the children of God." We believers will be recognized for what we really are—the children of God. What is hidden now by our corruptible bodies will be revealed in new, incorruptible bodies. The word used for "children" is *tékna* (5043), children having received the new birth from above (John 3:3, 7). Every child of God, regardless of his or her level of personal growth, will have this incorruptible body. This is the minimum promised to us, a tremendous prospect for believers. While we are suffering from weakness now, someday we will have incorruptible bodies.

Faith healers want all the benefits of the future right now. But Paul says, "We with patience wait for it" (Rom. 8:25). Faith healers do not want to wait, for they do not understand God's timing.

Romans 8:23 says that believers "have the firstfruits of the Spirit. . . ." We have our spiritual salvation here and now and forever. We are, however, "waiting for the adoption, to wit, the redemption of our body." It is coming. It is not yet here, but it gives us strength and hope as we await that day.

5

The Christian's Hope in Time of Sickness

The Bible gives believers hope even during the worst possible conditions we can experience here in our earthly life. This hope, however, is only for the Christian, not for those who have not received Jesus Christ as their Lord and Savior. There are only two classes of people: believers and unbelievers. When you close your eyes for the last time, you want to know what the future holds for you. Therefore, the most important thing a person must settle is his relationship to the Lord Jesus Christ.

Firstfruits Now . . .

The future of the believer is not the same as that of the unbeliever. One radical difference between the believer and the unbeliever is what the apostle Paul calls the "firstfruits." He says in Romans 8:23 that Christians ". . . have the firstfruits of the Spirit. . . ." We have spiritual rebirth. It is called the life of Christ, and we receive it the moment we believe. We begin to think and feel differently. "Firstfruits" in Greek is *aparchḗ* (536). It is only the start, the beginning. There is a continuation. We receive a new spirit, and we become a "new creation" (2 Cor. 5:17). *Kainḗ* (2537), new, means a qualitatively new creation.

Faster than lightening, God can change your spirit. All it takes is a turning to Christ in faith, and you can be made new spiritually, even if you are physically ill. This new spirit or new birth can be yours right now; it is the "firstfruit" of God's Spirit working in you.

. . . But Still Corruptible

But we all still have corruptible bodies, whether we are believers or unbelievers. A literal Greek rendering of 1 Corinthians 15:42 says, "It is sown in corruptibility but it is raised in incorruptibility." The believer is the subject spoken about here, but notice that his body is corruptible. We get wrinkles, gray hair, and so forth, just like unbelievers. The body is sown in weakness (*asthéneia* [769], lack of strength). You see, we all suffer from physical weaknesses. Just because we have the "firstfruits" does not mean that we are exempted from sickness or infirmities. Our body is sown a *psuchikós* (5591), a natural body. We are still connected to the earth in which we live.

Now some say today that when you become a Christian you can throw your medicines away. This is just not true. It is the preaching of a fanciful utopia. God is sovereign, and He can heal diseases, but it is His prerogative to do as He will.

There is a very good reason why you are not different physically from the unbeliever. The Bible's explanation comes to us through Paul in Romans 8. According to Paul, when Adam fell, he not only fell, but he dragged the whole creation down with him. Paul wrote, "For the creature [*ktísis* {2937}] was made subject to vanity, not willingly" (Rom. 8:20). Adam and Eve did not willingly submit themselves to God and, because of their disobedience, God subjected them and all of nature to corruption. Man made the choice to disobey, but he could not choose the consequences ("was made subject to vanity, not willingly"). God imposed the consequences ("but by reason of Him who has subjected the same in hope"). Notice, there is hope. If you became different physically right now, you would be like a "fish out of water." The environment would not be suitable for you. God must cancel out the effects of Adam's fall before you can live in an incorruptible body. So, do not believe those teachers who are telling you that you can toss away your medicine because you have been spiritually reborn.

In order, though, to have any hope in God's plan for the future, you must believe in the Lord Jesus Christ and become a child of God. Then you can claim God's promises for your future.

Our Profitable Death

Many believers are now suffering from sickness and disease. What separates them from unbelievers is that their spirits are reborn. What happens when the Christian dies?

Paul answers that question in Philippians 1:21 where he says, "For to me to live is Christ, and to die is gain." The Christian is consumed with one thought: How can I please the Lord Jesus Christ? The goal of the Christian ceases to be fame, power, or money, and becomes a life lived to honor Christ here on earth.

This is our goal—"to live is Christ." What happens at a Christian's death? Paul says, "to die is gain." The word "gain" means profit. It is to the believer's advantage to die. The only things lost are the temporal things of this world. The believer continues to live on in glory, and all the pain, struggles, tears, and corruption are left behind. Paul deals with this in 2 Corinthians 5. We, as believers, will put on a new form of identity when we are raised from the dead.

But the unbeliever does not have this hope at death. He has merely the prospect of terror after death. In Luke 16, Jesus told us what the unbeliever can expect. When Lazarus died he was gently taken to Abraham's bosom (v. 22). He had suffered from sores (v. 20) and could very well have been a leper. The rich man, however, went to Hades (v. 23), and Jesus says he "lifted up his eyes." So we know that his spirit had (non-physical) eyes of its own that could see after he died, and he was in torment. He had an easy life on earth, and his hard heart saw Lazarus suffering and yet he did nothing about it (vv. 19–21). So, what do unbelievers have to anticipate? Torment. It is a wise thing to examine yourself. Are you an unbeliever? It is an awful thing to die without hope.

Our Glorious Resurrection

The Bible tells us there is going to be a resurrection for both believers and unbelievers. In John 5:28 Jesus says, "Marvel not at this: for the hour is coming, in the which all that are in the graves shall hear His voice." The Lord is going to call both believers and unbelievers to rise from the dead. In John 5:29 it says, "they that have done good, unto the resurrection of life." This is for the believers.

The Christian will then be clothed in an incorruptible body (1 Cor. 15:42). He is not going to feel pain, sickness, or weakness anymore. It is a glorious experience to which we as believers can look forward. Our bodies are now dishonorable, but then they will be raised in glory (1 Cor. 15:43).

The Christian has been redeemed in his spirit and will be redeemed in his body—both components will be redeemed when God so determines. When the unbeliever is raised, he will be given a body that will eternally suffer, and that without hope (Rev. 14:11).

Our Coming Adoption

Paul says in Romans 8:23, "We ourselves groan within ourselves, waiting for the adoption [*huiothesía* {5206}]." When we die there is not only the judgment as to whether we have believed or not that we will experience; we will also be judged on how we lived our lives, whether in the body of Christ or estranged from Him. God will look on our obedience or disobedience.

Some Christians have been real problems, a real nuisance to the family of God. Could you have been one of them? This will be determined on the resurrection day. When a person becomes a believer, he becomes a child of God. The word is *téknon* (5043), translated "child," and it comes from *tíktō* (5088) which means to give birth. There are varieties of children. Some obey God more than others. Some grow up. Some remain babies. The other word used for believers is "sons" of God. This word is *huiós* (5207). In John 1:12 it reads, "But as many as received Him, to them gave He power to become the sons of God," but "sons" here is *tékna.* We become infants, but we grow in increased obedience. Each one is to grow into a *huiós.* We are to grow up!

Now the word "adoption" in Romans 8:23 is *huiothesía.* The first part comes from *huiós,* son, and the second part comes from the verb *títhēmi* (5087), to place. Our adoption, then, answers the question as to where we fit. We are going to be judged on how we "fit" in the family of God. Did we obey or disobey? How frequent was our obedience? We will be rewarded based on our obedience to the Lord.

Of course, this has no bearing at all for the unbeliever. He will have gone through the resurrection of damnation and have no rewards.

Our New Home

God will make a new heaven and a new earth for resurrected believers. Revelation 21:1 says, "I saw a new heaven and a new earth." It is not merely "another" earth. The word used is *kainós,* qualitatively new, another of a different kind; not *néos* (3501), another of the same kind. Thus it will be an entirely new and different earth and heaven. Remember that only the believer shares in this new heaven and earth. Also remember that a person's spiritual life can begin immediately. You can be physically dying right now, but spiritual life can become yours instantly by receiving Christ as your Savior.

Our God-Given Eagerness

So, if you are a believer, you have the "firstfruits" in your spirit, but you live in a corruptible body in a corruptible world, and it is not totally satisfying. It is a God-allowed discomfort with the present situation.

We are waiting for our adoption and resurrection (Rom. 8:23). The Greek word is *apekdéchomai* (553) and means that I expect something from the hand of God. It is as though I am standing on my tiptoes with my hands outstretched! We are eagerly awaiting "the redemption of our body" (Rom. 8:23). The word "redemption" is *apolútrōsis* (629) and it is used for the redemption of our spirits also. *Apó* (575) means "from" and *lútrōsis* (3085) means something you are liberated from. We will all be liberated from our aches, pains, sickness, sin, and so forth Our God-given eagerness for this redemption of our bodies is a great hope for all Christians.

Remember, though, this hope is only for the believer. The unbeliever has no right to claim it for himself. Have you put your faith in the Lord Jesus Christ?

6

Paul and the Healing Ministry

Paul understood very well and taught that a believer's body and an unbeliever's body are both corruptible. Both waste away until we die. The basic verse in the Word of God that shows what our attitude toward illness should be is found in Romans 8:28. We know that God is our Father and nothing happens haphazardly to His people. He works all things together for our good.

We must examine our attitude toward sickness. We must ask, Lord, what do you want to accomplish in me through this sickness?

Hope of Future Reward

Both believers and unbelievers suffer illnesses, but what gives the Christian the ability to say, Thank you, Lord? It is because we have eternal life now. We have the life of God within our hearts that enables us to have peace and joy even in trouble.

This eternal life is a present reality according to the Lord Jesus Christ. He said in John 3:16 that he who believes in Him has eternal life. But we also have a future reward to which we look forward. Jesus said in Mark 10:29–30, "Verily, I say unto you, there is no man that hath left house, or brethren, or sisters, or father, or mother, or wife, or children, or lands, for My sake, and the gospel's, but he shall receive . . . in the world to come eternal life." We have it the moment we believe, and there is a sense in which it will be given even more fully in the future.

Since we know that the Lord sovereignly allows sickness in the believer's life, he looks at his sickness and knows there will be a reward for his patient endurance.

Certainly the believer will and should ask the Lord to heal him, but he wants above all to conform his life to his Father's will. He knows that his reward will come, and that is enough for now to cheer and encourage him.

Seeing Divine Intervention

A believer also knows that God is intervening in his life in a good way, even in sickness and trouble. In the Beatitudes (Matt. 5:3–11), we have the word "blessed" (*makários* [3107]). It means to have God within you here and now. The other word for "blessed" is used in Matthew 25:34 where Jesus said, "Come, ye blessed of My Father, inherit the kingdom." That word is *eulogēménoi* (2127), which is a totally different word. It means those spoken well of by God, or those in whose lives God intervened and blessed.

Jesus and His People Care

Jesus identifies Himself with the sufferings of His people. Matthew 25:35 says, "I was hungry and you gave Me something to eat" (a.t.). Jesus identifies with the hungry, not the filled. Yes, we can be hungry, but we know that Jesus is fully satisfying.

"I was sick." "Sick" is *asthenéō* (770). Jesus identifies with the sick. He was never sick Himself, yet He identifies with His God-intervened ones.

Not only does Jesus sympathize, but we are to do the same. Certainly this was the apostle Paul's attitude when he wrote in 2 Corinthians 11:29: "Who is weak, and I am not weak?" This word for "weak" is *asthenéō,* which means to be sick or ill. It is being without strength. In most cases, it is translated "sick." Paul believed it was possible to be a believer and be sick at the same time. In fact, he was the "sick apostle" (2 Cor. 12:7–10), and he gloried in that fact (2 Cor. 11:30).

Paul and Jesus not only sympathized with sickness, Jesus specifically says that there are rewards for our sympathy toward the sick among us (Matt. 25:40). So, we are encouraged and even commanded to visit the sick, not condemning them during their weakness, but ministering to them, and in so doing, ministering to Christ.

Demand-Free Living

A misleading teaching of the gospel today is that a follower of Christ should have an easy life. It is the idea that whatever one wants, he can have, whether it is fame, money, or riches.

That was not the attitude of one of the greatest saints who ever lived on earth, the apostle Paul. What was Paul's greatest desire for the church? He recorded that in 2 Corinthians 11:2: "For I am jealous over you with godly jealousy: for I have espoused you to one husband, that I may present you as a chaste virgin to Christ." Purity was Paul's greatest desire for the church.

Paul declared that he ministered "in weariness and painfulness, in watchings often, in hunger and thirst" (2 Cor. 11:27). Here we see no demands for wages, no clock-watching, no set time to minister, and no demanding of his rights. Paul did not demand that his physical problem be healed. He had asked three times (2 Cor. 12:8), and the Lord told him, "My grace is sufficient for thee: for My strength is made perfect in weakness" (v. 9). Paul was told by the Lord, No, but I will help you live with your weakness, because I get the glory out of it.

Paul's attitude was to be Christ's servant.

Caution in Weariness

When we are sick or ill we are also vulnerable. There are some who are preaching—or pretending to preach—the health and wealth gospel, and their lives are not what Paul would endorse.

There are those who make claims for wealth, fame, and health, and they are nothing like the great apostle Paul. Paul wrote, "But I fear, lest by any means, as the serpent beguiled Eve . . . so your minds should be corrupted from the simplicity that is in Christ. For if he that cometh preacheth another Jesus . . . or another gospel . . . ye might well bear with him" (2 Cor. 11:3–4). But Paul himself had weaknesses, needs, and much he could have complained about (2 Cor. 11:23–33).

Now we know that Paul did fantastic miracles of healing (see Acts 19:11), so much so that some were healed by Paul's "aprons" (KJV: "handkerchiefs," v. 12). These were long cloths which men tied around their waist to use to wipe away the sweat or as a towel when needed. There were some in Ephesus who tried to imitate the apostle Paul. Paul did not use these "aprons" for healing, nor did he authorize their use. There is a principle here: God can achieve His purpose even when the means used are not authorized.

In this same chapter we see seven vagabond Jewish exorcists who decided to try to imitate the apostle's ministry (v. 13), but they did not fare too well (v. 16)! And here we have another principle: not everybody who preaches is a true minister of the gospel, and some may believe in Christ in spite of the fact that the preacher is unsaved. These unsaved exorcists had no relationship to Jesus or Paul (v. 15).

A third principle to sharpen our caution is to know that healing is not a matter of articles of clothing or other material things. If it were, Paul would have sent "aprons" to his friends Timothy and Epaphroditus when they were sick. The healing power is not in material items, but in the hands of Jesus.

So, be wary in your sickness, and do not be vulnerable to what sounds so alluring but is false.

Submitting to God's Sovereignty

Jesus, who was the only One with unrestricted power to heal, did not always choose to heal. He chose not to do miracles in Nazareth (Matt. 13:58), and He only healed one man at the pool of Bethesda (John 5:2–9). In His sovereignty, He limited His healing.

But as we study the New Testament, it is evident that Paul could not practice healing at any time he wanted or with respect to whomever he wanted.

Paul himself was sick. "Who is weak [sick], and I am not?" (2 Cor. 11:29). "Weak" or "sick" is that word *asthenéō.* Paul was a sickly person, probably with eye disease and perhaps malaria, and for this he was criticized. His enemies said, "His bodily presence is weak" (2 Cor. 10:10). Again, "weak" is *asthenḗs* (772), sickly. This shows us that it is not how physically strong or how eloquent a person is that is important, but that God can use his weakness or strength for His glory. The greatest apostle who ever lived was sickly.

Of all the New Testament writers, Paul alone mentions gifts (*charísmata* [5486]) and especially the gifts of healings (1 Cor. 12:9). What is the meaning of *charísmata?* It is the instantaneous enablement by the Triune God—God the Father, God the Son, and God the Holy Spirit—for a believer to do something out of the ordinary and beyond human possibility in order to accomplish a purpose He has designed.

In Ephesus (Acts 19), Paul did not have unrestricted power to heal everyone. He never claimed to be a healer. God could use Paul to heal when it was His will to accomplish His own eternal purpose, but it was selective. God is sovereign. He decides if and when a person is to be healed.

There were people Paul could not heal. He could not heal himself (2 Cor. 12:7–10). He said, "I will not glory, but in mine infirmities" (v. 5). Again, *asthéneia* (769) is used.

Paul could not heal Timothy, his "dearly beloved son" (2 Tim. 1:2). He advised Timothy to drink a little wine and stop drinking the water (1 Tim. 5:23). Although Paul could not heal him, there is little doubt that he prayed to the Lord that He would. Paul did not send an "apron." He advised using the medicinal means available. We also should use available means.

Paul also could not heal Trophimus (2 Tim. 4:20), and Epaphroditus, who almost died (Phil. 2:25–28), was another one Paul could not heal.

There has never been a human being on earth, no matter how great, who could heal anybody he wished at anytime. Our attitude should be like Paul's—we should submit to God's ways even when they appear to discomfort us and the ones we love.

7

Was There Healing in the Atonement?

It is a wonderful thing to discern the deeper truths of God's Word. No one should settle for the easy, simplistic solutions. There are some preachers who say that God will do anything at any time for anybody who simply believes, but we have already seen that God is sovereign as to when and how He will work. We must be honest and careful as we study the Word of God.

Man's Greatest Problem

We know that at Adam's fall in the Garden of Eden (Gen. 3:1–8) all mankind fell in him. He disobeyed a clear, simple command and reaped the consequences of that disobedience (Rom. 5:12). Death came to man.

Man's death was first alienation or separation from his Creator (Gen. 3:8). From a condition of close fellowship, man fell and then tried to hide from God. But not only that, physical death was also his punishment—inevitable though not immediate (Gen. 3:19).

Christ, the Problem Solver

God had to seek out Adam. The central point of the Bible is that Jesus Christ is God incarnate, the seeker of the lost. As John 1:14 says, "the Word was made [became] flesh" Why? Because if the Son of God had not become man, there would be no totally adequate sacrifice for our sins. That was the reason for His incarnation.

Hebrews 9:22 clearly teaches that "without shedding of blood there is no remission." Jesus shed His blood because the justice of God required a holy sacrifice, and Jesus was willing to take our punishment, for "the wages of sin is death" (Rom. 6:23). That is what Paul meant in Romans 3:26 when he said, "that He might be just, and the justifier of him which believeth in Jesus." Christ's merciful, sacrificial death took away the just wrath of God against the sinner (Eph. 2:3).

This is God's plan of salvation—that a person repent and look to Christ in simple faith as the all-sufficient sacrifice for his sin. This is the concept of atonement found in the Old Testament. The Greek equivalent for the Hebrew word is *exilasmós* (n.f.). The word comes from *híleōs* (2436) which means to provide for the redemption of man.

But what did this redemption entail? Was it primarily to redeem our spirits, or was it to liberate man from sickness and disease? We will examine that, and, although the word "redemption" focuses primarily on the spiritual dimension, no part of man's nature is excluded from the redemption provided by Christ on the cross.

There are three words we will do well to study: *lútrōsis* (3085), *lutróō* (3084), and *apolútrōsis* (629).

Lútrōsis

Lútrōsis is the rescuing of man from the consequence of his own disobedience and choices. It is the paying of a ransom—not to Satan into whose power man fell (Col. 1:13), but to the Father to satisfy the righteous requirement of His unchanging moral law.

The first New Testament reference to *lútrōsis* is found in Luke 1:68. This is the Song of Zecharias when he learned that he and his wife, Elizabeth, were going to be the parents of John the Baptist. Zecharias said, "He hath visited and redeemed His people." Notice that this is a spiritual redemption.

Another reference of *lútrōsis* is found in Luke 2:38 where we find Anna in the temple when Jesus was dedicated by His mother and stepfather and "spake of Him to all them that looked for redemption in Jerusalem." Again, this is a spiritual redemption. Also notice that this spiritual redemption of Israel has not yet come. Here we have something predicted to occur based on what Jesus has now accomplished on the cross.

Hebrews 9:12 has the third usage of *lútrōsis* and declares that the Lord Jesus "entered in once into the holy place, having obtained eternal redemption for us." This is a spiritual and eternal redemption. Jesus referred to this when He said, "Your father Abraham rejoiced to see My day: and he saw it, and was glad" (John 8:56). Abraham looked forward by faith to the sacrifice of Christ, and we look back to that very same cross. No one is saved any other way.

Lutróō

Lútrōsis is a derivative from *lutróō* meaning to redeem, which is found three times in the New Testament. Its first occurrence is in Luke 24:21 where two disciples, unaware of the Lord's resurrection, related their sadness when they said, "But we trusted that it had been He which should have redeemed Israel." Here we see that the redemption was primarily from sin. There was not even a hint here of physical healing.

Its second occurrence is in Titus 2:14 where Paul states that Jesus Christ "gave Himself for us, that He might redeem us from all iniquity, and purify unto Himself a peculiar people, zealous of good works." Here Paul is saying that the purpose of Christ's redemptive work was primarily spiritual. Paul does not even mention illness or sickness. The death of Christ does include provision for the healing of the total person, but that is not the primary emphasis. Paul's emphasis is on our moral/spiritual condition. "Iniquity" is *anomía* (458) which is lawlessness. We run from God and His laws when we are unredeemed, but when we are born again, we want to obey God's commandments and live in fellowship with Him. Anyone who does not desire that pure life has never experienced the work of redemption.

The last occurrence of this word is in 1 Peter 1:18 where Peter said that we "were not redeemed with corruptible things, as silver and gold, from your vain conversation received by tradition from your fathers." The New American Standard Bible translates "vain conversation" as "futile way of life." Peter is concerned with the spiritual lives of his readers. This is a spiritual redemption.

Apolútrōsis

The third word is an intensified form of *lútrōsis* meaning complete redemption. There is a sense in which, even now, we possess complete redemption.

Hebrews 9:15 says that Jesus is "the mediator of the new testament, that by means of [His] death, for the redemption of the transgressions that were under the first testament, they which are called might receive the promise of eternal inheritance." "Redemption" here is *apolútrōsis.* This redemption deals with "transgressions" (*parabáseis* [3847]). This is a serious breaking of the known will of God. The reason why Jesus' death was complete redemption is because His blood is superior beyond comparison to the blood of "goats and calves" (Heb. 9:12). The Old Testament sacrifices were incomplete—a mere sign of what was to come. The blood of Christ accomplishes *apolútrōsis,* complete redemption.

Another occurrence is found in 1 Corinthians 1:30: "Christ Jesus, who of God is made unto us wisdom, and righteousness, and sanctification, and redemption." This is also a spiritual redemption. It is complete spiritual restoration. Since He is the one who gives us this complete redemption, there is nothing we can add, and so Paul could declare, "He that glorieth, let him glory in the Lord" (v. 31).

Apolútrōsis also occurs in Ephesians 1:7. The apostle wrote, "In whom we have redemption through His blood, the forgiveness of sins" Here the emphasis is clearly on the forgiveness of our sins.

Again we find the word used in Colossians 1:14. It is an exact repetition of Ephesians 1:7. This is again a spiritual redemption for Christians. Paul had just written, "Who hath delivered us from the power of darkness, and hath translated us into the kingdom of His dear Son" (v. 13). So, the believer in the Lord Jesus Christ has the same physical body, but is linked to God. That is why Paul wrote, "We know that all things work together for good to them that love God" (Rom. 8:28).

Romans 3:24 also has the word *apolútrōsis.* Paul wrote, "Being justified freely by His grace through the redemption that is in Christ Jesus." No physical healing is evident at all in this passage, for it is a continuation of verse 23: "For all have sinned and come short of the glory of God." The forgiveness of the guilt of mankind's sins was accomplished completely through the cross of Christ. We cannot add a thing to it. Neither is it necessary for Christ to ever sacrifice Himself again (Heb. 9:25–28; 1 Pet. 3:18).

So these three Greek words, *lútrōsis, lutróō,* and *apolútrōsis,* place the emphasis on the spiritual dimension of the redemption of Christ on the cross. As we have them, though, there are hints of more to come.

Our Future Redemption

Our redemption is complete now in the sense that it fulfilled the focus of the Old Testament sacrifices, and Jesus need never sacrifice Himself again, and we can add nothing to it. There is a sense, however, where *apolútrōsis* refers to a future completion of our redemption.

We currently have "the firstfruits of the Spirit, even we ourselves groan within ourselves, waiting for the adoption, to wit, the redemption of our body" (Rom. 8:23). Our "firstfruits of the Spirit" is our spiritually complete redemption, but our bodies are still often sick and weak. They are corruptible. We still suffer from *asthéneia* (769), weakness or sickness. We do not despair, however, even in illnesses which the Lord permits.

We are "waiting for" our complete bodily redemption, and if we are still waiting, it is obvious that we do not possess it yet. When will this possession happen? When the Lord returns for His people at the Rapture. Only then will we be liberated from the consequences of sin in our bodies. This is the hope of the believer.

Another use of *apolútrōsis* is found in Luke 21:28: "And when these things begin to come to pass, then look up, and lift up your heads; for your redemption draweth nigh." Jesus is clearly telling us that our complete redemption (spirit, soul, and body) will happen at His Second Coming (see Luke 21:25–27).

Ephesians 1:14 uses the word *apolútrōsis* where the apostle wrote, "which is the earnest of our inheritance until the redemption of the purchased possession." Our spiritual redemption is now the down payment of our complete redemption that is yet to come. The "purchased possession" is *peripoíēsis* (4047), meaning to envelop us with gentle care. He is all around us. We may go through times of sickness, but that does not mean that God has stopped watching over us.

The final use of *apolútrōsis* is in Ephesians 4:30, where we are told to "grieve not the Holy Spirit of

God, whereby ye are sealed unto the day of redemption." When we believed, we were baptized in the Holy Spirit. We were marked as God's own. This is a mystical, spiritual union that exists between the believer and the Lord Jesus Christ. So we now have our "sealing," and in the future at Jesus' Second Coming, we shall have our complete bodily redemption.

Life-Changing Truths

Now, what we have examined in these words has a great influence on our daily lives. These are words which strengthen us in our faith. In the great "faith chapter" of Hebrews 11, we see how powerful our faith can be.

In verse 31 it says, "By faith the harlot Rahab perished not with them that believed not." God can lift a harlot up and make her His holy child. She was redeemed. Why? Because of the eternal redemption of Jesus Christ. She did not perish like those "that believed not," although she eventually died. There is a tremendous difference between the death of the believer and the nonbeliever. Like Rahab, everyone who wants to die as a Christian believer must decide for Christ in this life.

Hebrews 11:33 says that these people "subdued kingdoms." We can subdue kingdoms. They "wrought righteousness." We can replace our evil and unjust ways with righteousness and justice through the presence of Christ in our lives and bring about righteousness in our homes and communities.

Finally, note Hebrews 11:34: "out of weakness were made strong." Out of *astheneías*, out of our sicknesses, we can serve Jesus Christ. When you are laid flat on your back in illness, you can know that the Lord is with you and that someday all the pain will be forgotten. You will have a new body. This is the better resurrection. This is truth that transforms.

8

Infirmities or Weaknesses

There has been a lot of misunderstanding regarding Matthew 8:16–17: "When the even was come, they brought unto Him many that were possessed with devils: and He cast out the spirits with His word, and healed all that were sick; That it might be fulfilled which was spoken by Isaiah the prophet, saying, Himself took our infirmities, and bare our sicknesses."

There are two kinds of people referred to here: the "demonized," if we translate literally, and "those who had it badly" (*kakō̃s* [2560] *échontas* [2192]), not the "sick." Jesus performed *therapeúō* (2323), which means that He took care of their symptoms. He ministered to them. This was a direct fulfillment of a prophecy from Isaiah 53:4. Now, let us examine in depth the key phrases of Matthew 8:17 to see what it really teaches.

"Our Infirmities"

The word "infirmity" can mean either a physical infirmity or a spiritual infirmity. The word is *astheneías*

(769), which means lack of strength. One of the important principles in word studies in the Bible is to recognize the concept that a word can have more than one meaning depending on the context in which it is used. A student must not take a word with several meanings and force it to have the same meaning every time it is used.

Romans 5:6 sheds some light on the word *asthéneia* (770). In fact, the entire book of Romans is a great theological dictionary for the Christian faith. Paul wrote of a time "when we were yet without strength." The words "without strength" is *asthenḗs* (772). Does this refer to physical or spiritual sickness? He continued, "in due time Christ died for the ungodly." The context here clearly shows that Paul was talking of spiritual issues, not physical issues. The word "ungodly" is *asebḗs* (765) and means to be godless, without fear or reverence for God. It thus defines for us *asthéneia* (sickness) in this context. This is further confirmed in Romans 5:8 where Paul said, "While we were yet sinners, Christ died for us." *Asthéneia* here means that we were spiritually sick.

There are other passages where *asthéneia* (sickness) refers to physical illness or sickness. John recorded the healing of a lame man at the Pool of Bethesda (John 5:3–18). He wrote, "In these lay a great multitude of impotent folk" (v. 3). The word for "impotent" is *asthenoúntōn,* a form of *asthéneia.* One man had his infirmity thirty-eight years and Jesus healed him (v. 9).

There is a hint here that this man's illness was a result of some personal sin, because Jesus warned him, "Behold, thou art made whole: sin no more, lest a worse thing come unto thee" (v. 14). In a very real sense, all sickness has sprung from sin somewhere, either from our own or, originally, from Adam's.

Jesus had asked this man if he wanted to be made "whole." The word for "whole" is *hugiḗs* (5199) from which we get our word "hygienic." Jesus cleansed him physically from his *asthéneia.*

So we can see that the word *asthéneia* can be either spiritual weakness, as in Romans 5:8, or physical weakness, depending on the context in which it occurs.

The Suffering Servant

In order to determine whether we should understand *asthéneia* in Matthew 8:17 as referring to spiritual or physical illness, we should carefully examine the entire chapter in which the verse is found.

Isaiah 53:1–2—which is the frame for Isaiah 53:4 quoted in Matthew 8:17—clearly points to the Lord Jesus Christ: "Who hath believed our report? and to whom is the arm of the Lord revealed? For He shall grow up before Him as a tender plant, and as a root out of a dry ground: He hath no form nor comeliness; and when we shall see Him, there is no beauty that we should desire Him." Evidently Jesus was not the handsome person we have pictured for us today!

"He is despised and rejected of men: a man of sorrows, and acquainted with grief" (v. 3). This is a clear description of our Lord Jesus' life here on earth. "And we hid as it were our faces from Him; He was despised, and we esteemed Him not." The vast multitude turned on Him and even one of the Twelve betrayed Him.

Now we come to Isaiah 53:4: "Surely He hath borne our griefs, and carried our sorrows: yet we did esteem Him stricken, smitten of God, and afflicted." Does this mean that since Jesus took our griefs, we do not grieve anymore? Do you know of any believer, do you know of any saint of God who is without grief? He identified with, but did not remove our griefs when He suffered on the cross. That is an important point to keep in mind.

Continuing in the passage, "But He was wounded for our transgressions, He was bruised for our iniquities: the chastisement of our peace was upon Him; and with His stripes we are healed" (v. 5). This verse, which is quoted in 1 Peter 2:24, is often misunderstood because people see the word "healed" and immediately think of physical healing. The Hebrew word is *rapha* (7495, OT), which refers to a total restoration to the condition in which God first created us. The emphasis in this verse is on our spiritual sickness. We are sinners. We commit "transgressions" and "iniquities," and so this verse is primarily speaking of our spiritual redemption.

Again, "All we like sheep have gone astray; we have turned every one to his own way; and the Lord has laid on Him the iniquity of us all" (v. 6). Notice that the human race fled from the Lord. We all do what Adam and Eve did after they sinned. For them, and us, it is primarily a spiritual problem.

Our identification of Jesus as the focus of this chapter is confirmed by verses 7 and 8, for this is the passage from which the Ethiopian eunuch was reading when Philip spoke to him (Acts 8:32–33). Philip identified the Suffering Servant as Jesus after the eunuch asked, "I pray thee, of whom speaketh the prophet this? of himself, or of some other man?" (Acts 8:34).

In verse 8, Isaiah wrote, "He was taken from prison and from judgment: and who shall declare His generation? for He was cut off out of the land of the living: for the transgression of my people was He stricken." Jesus was not stricken primarily for our health, but for our sins.

"And He made His grave with the wicked, and with the rich in His death; because He had done no violence, neither was any deceit in His mouth" (v. 9). After our Lord's death His body was requested by Joseph of Arimathaea, a rich man, and placed in a new tomb (Matt. 27:57–60).

Further, "Yet it pleased the Lord to bruise Him; He hath put Him to grief: when Thou shalt make His soul an offering for sin" (v. 10). An offering for health? No, for sin.

And verse 11 closes with, "By His knowledge shall my righteous servant justify many; for He shall bear their iniquities." This sounds so much like the apostle Paul speaking (see Rom. 5:18–19). Sin is the emphasis of this entire chapter in Isaiah. Jesus Christ came primarily to die for sin.

You see, it is not a responsible method of approaching the Scriptures to take Isaiah 53:5 to refer to physical healing while the whole chapter refers to the "infirmities" that Jesus took upon Himself for the sins of the people.

"And Bare Our Sicknesses"

In most translations the word "our" in Matthew 8:17 is italicized. This indicates that it was inserted by the translators and is not part of the original text. As we have noted, the word for "sicknesses" is *nósous* (3554), "diseases."

The Lord Jesus on the cross took all diseases, and the day will come when there will be no diseases at all. That is why Paul wrote, "having made peace through the blood of His cross, by him to reconcile all things unto Himself" (Col. 1:20).

In the Isaiah quote that "He bore our diseases," the word "bore" is *bastázō* (941), to take up and hold. It comes from the Greek word *básis* (939), from which we have the English word "basis." Jesus tasted the ultimate consequences of disease and sickness, which is death so that one day He can give us a body that cannot be affected by any disease whatsoever.

Our Current Hope

If Jesus "took" our weaknesses in the sense that we do not have them anymore, why would Paul write, "For though He was crucified through weakness, yet He liveth by the power of God. For we also are weak in Him, but we shall live with Him by the power of God toward you" (2 Cor. 13:4)?

We are weak (*astheneís*) in spite of the fact that He is in us and we in Him. Paul wrote in the present tense because it is a present, continuing reality. We are still besieged by human frailties. Jesus "took" them—He identified with us—yet we still have them. But someday we will not. Someday we will be incorruptible (1 Cor. 15:54).

The Lord can heal anyone at any time if it is within His sovereign will to do so. When ill, we encourage you to pray to the Lord to be healed. If it is not His will to heal, then we know that someday we will be given a body that no disease whatsoever is going to affect (Rom. 8:23).

So, the first part of Matthew 8:17 ("He Himself took our infirmities") speaks of His identification with humanity in His incarnation. He took a pure human nature and human body to Himself. The second portion ("and bore the sicknesses") speaks of complete liberation from disease for His people when we are changed into His likeness at our resurrection.

9

What Did Jesus Cancel on the Cross?

We have seen that many people want to use Matthew 8:17, "Himself took our infirmities, and bore our sicknesses," to mean that we should never experience illness. In their interpretation, the healing referred to is taken to be physical healing.

First Peter 2:24 is a parallel Scripture to Matthew 8:17: "Who His own self bore our sins in His own body on the tree, that we, being dead to sins, should live unto righteousness: by whose stripes ye were healed." Does this verse mean that, based on what the Lord Jesus Christ did on the cross, we need not suffer sicknesses any longer?

In order to answer that question properly, we have to dig deeply into God's Word and not be content with mere surface evaluation. We believe in the verbal inspiration of the Scriptures, and that means that every word was "breathed-out" by the Holy Spirit. As the apostle Paul said, "All scripture is given by inspiration of God" (2 Tim. 3:16). That puts a responsibility on us to carefully study the text.

The English translation of the Greek New Testament does not always give us the shades of meaning which the original languages convey. For example, there are three verbs which are used relative to this study, yet our English translation does not reflect that diversity. Two are in Matthew 8:17 where we have *lambánō* (2983) for "took" and *bastázō* (941) for "bore." Remember that *lambánō* does not mean that our Lord removed weakness (*asthéneia* [770]) from us, but that He took upon Himself human weakness in His incarnation. *Bastázō* (coming from *básis* [939], the "very bottom") means that He bore them so that they become more tolerable for the Christian because he has a hope beyond this life. It does not mean we are immune from sickness, but that we glorify God as we go through it.

We are not trying to be overly particular as we examine 1 Peter 2:24, "who His own self bore our sins in His own body on the tree, that we, being dead to sins, should live unto righteousness: by whose stripes ye were healed"; but we need to look at it phrase by phrase to carefully glean the true meaning of this text.

"Who His Own Self Bore"

The third verb is *anaphérō* (399) from *aná* (303), up, and *phérō* (5342), to carry or bring. Jesus not only stooped down to us and took our infirmities, but He also took our sins and lifted them up and away. This is what Jesus did on the cross. We can comprehend this better when we compare key references such as Isaiah 53 and Matthew 8:17.

Let us be honest. Believers do get sick. No physician would claim that a Christian body was physiologically different from a non-Christian body. The context of 1 Peter 2:24 helps us to determine the overall message which Peter is bringing.

Did Jesus suffer when He took upon Himself our sicknesses so that ours are cancelled out? Peter wrote, "For even hereunto were ye called: because Christ also suffered for us . . ." (1 Pet. 2:21). That was intrinsic in His death on the cross. He took flesh upon Himself in order to be punished for our sins in our place. He did not eliminate our diseases; He was sacrificed in our place.

Peter continued, "leaving us an example, that ye should follow in His steps" (v. 21). Jesus did not suffer deservedly, but He did suffer voluntarily and vicariously. How unlike Him we are if we always want to eliminate our suffering. That is not following "in His steps."

"Our Sins in His Own Body on the Tree"

There is a definite connection between Matthew 8:17 and 1 Peter 2:24. That connection is their mutual use of Isaiah 53 as their source and meaning. This helps us to understand the main theme of Peter's message.

As we saw before, Matthew 8:17 refers to Isaiah 53:4–5 which says, "He hath borne our griefs, and carried our sorrows" (v. 4), and we learned that these griefs and sorrows are primarily the burdens of our sins.

Isaiah continued, "Yet we did esteem Him stricken, smitten of God, and afflicted." Now keep this carefully in mind—it was the Father who sent Jesus to the cross. Paul wrote, "Who was delivered for our offenses, and was raised again for our justification" (Rom. 4:25). In the middle of our problems, we must remember that man can do nothing except as God gives permission. Neither can any disease attack us without His permission. This is how we follow "in His steps."

In the middle of His trial, Jesus said to Pilate, "Thou couldest have no power at all against Me, except it were given thee from above" (John 19:11). Jesus was always aware of his Father's control over everything.

Isaiah said He would make "His grave with the wicked" (53:9). He was buried with the wicked, but as Peter said, "Who did no sin, neither was guile found in his mouth" (1 Pet. 2:22), which Isaiah had also said when he prophesied, "He had done no violence" (53:9). Jesus was buried with the wicked, but He was not wicked Himself.

First Peter 2:23 says, "When He was reviled, reviled not again," which is parallel to Isaiah's "He opened not His mouth" (53:7).

There is no doubt that 1 Peter 2:21–24 directly echoes Isaiah 53, just as does Matthew 8:17. Since we have previously established that Isaiah 53 refers not to physical healing, but to spiritual healing, we conclude that Peter's message is also focused primarily on our spiritual healing.

"That We, Being Dead to Sin"

Now notice that Peter expressly tells us that the Lord Jesus bore our sins. Peter does not say a word about our sicknesses. The purpose or result of this action is that He made us "dead" to sin. One word for "dead" is *apogenómenoi* (581) from *apogínomai* (n.f. in this form) and refers to a moral relationship to sin of such a kind that the molding of the character by sin ceases.

What does it mean to be dead to sin? It means that sin does not have reigning power over us anymore. We have "remaining sin" but not "reigning sin."

Hebrews 9:26–28 sheds some important light on this subject. The author of Hebrews wrote, "But now once in the end of the world hath He appeared to put away sin" (v. 26). This is the primary purpose of the Lord Jesus' coming to die for us. Those who say that now that they are believers, they have no more sin or sicknesses, are guilty of very simplistic thinking.

Hebrews 9:27 says, "And as it is appointed unto men once to die, but after this the judgment." The judgment referred to here is for the unbeliever. The believer's sin has been canceled out. For believers, there is only one death for sin—Jesus' death. We will have a judgment, but it will be for our works. But the unbeliever remains condemned unless he believes, for as Jesus said, "He that believeth on Him is not condemned: but he that believeth not is condemned *already*, because he has not believed in the name of the only begotten Son of God" (John 3:18).

In Hebrews 9:28 the word "bear" occurs and is the same word *anaphérō* used in 1 Peter 2:24. Jesus stooped low to carry away our sins so that the Father could justly forgive us. He could go to the Father and say, The sin for this man, for this woman, who has become a believer, has been fully paid for by Me. Do not count this sin against them.

There are many people whose sins have been canceled. This is why Jesus can say to the Father, "Behold, I and the children which God hath given Me"

(Heb. 2:13). The death of Christ was a cancellation of our sin. He is our designated sin-bearer. Outside of Him, there is no hope.

"Should Live unto Righteousness"

There are some who say that because Jesus Christ died for our sins, Peter is teaching here that we can live a sinless life, just as we should live a "sickless" life.

Again, the context of 1 Peter 2:24 helps us. Verse 22 says, "Who did no sin, neither was guile found in His mouth." The issue is this: if Christ committed no sin, does that enable us, because of His death, not to sin anymore?

The letter of 1 John gives us biblical insight into this question. First John 2:1 says, "My little children, these things write I unto you, that you sin not." The verb for "sin" is *hamartánō* (264), which is an aorist subjunctive. This means, "that you may not commit one single sin." While we are still in this frail, sinful body, the goal set before us will still be not to sin one single time.

In the same verse, John continued, "And if any man sin, we have an advocate with the Father, Jesus Christ the righteous." We cannot say that now that we have been forgiven, we can do our own pleasure. Paul's response to that idea is "God forbid" (Rom. 6:2).

Jesus is our "advocate," our *paráklētos* (3875), one called, beside us. He is the universe's best lawyer. He pleads our case to the Father by His blood shed for our sins. That is why John adds, "And He is the propitiation for our sins" (1 John 2:2). Even if we sin just once, we miss the mark God has set for us, but our heavenly Lawyer pleads for us.

It is important to note that in 1 John 3:9 where John wrote, "Whosoever is born of God doth not commit sin . . . he cannot sin . . . ," that *hamartánō* is in the present tense. There will be an increased awareness of sin in the believer's life, but he is not habitually living in sin.

Peter clearly tells us that Jesus "did no sin" (1 Pet. 2:22). The Greek construction here means that He absolutely, in no way sinned. He always lived in complete accordance with the Father's will.

Our goal is that we "should live unto righteousness," but we are not little gods nor little Jesus'. We still have sin in our lives, and we still have sicknesses.

"By Whose Stripes Ye Were Healed"

This is the point where much controversy arises. Some take it to mean that because Jesus bore our sins, we no longer suffer either sins' guilt or sickness. We have already seen that Jesus' shed blood and death paid the price for our sins, but does the healing referred to here also mean that He took our sickness so that we are no longer prone to physical illness?

The last phrase in 1 Peter 2:24 is a quote from Isaiah 53:5, and as we have already established, "healed" in Isaiah 53 means to be saved from the condemnation and power of sin.

The Greek verb "healed" is *iáomai* (2390) and means a restoration to the healthy condition in which God created us. The usage or context of the word determines its meaning.

If we turn to Matthew 13, we find a passage that gives us insight into this word. Jesus had just delivered the Parable of the Sower, and His disciples had asked him why He used parables to teach. Jesus answered by quoting from Isaiah 6:8 and then said, "For this people's heart is waxed gross, and their ears are dull of hearing, and their eyes they have closed" (v. 15). Does Jesus mean that they have cholesterol problems, or physical deafness, or cataracts or glaucoma?

No, obviously not, because He continued, "lest at any time they should see with their eyes, and hear with their ears, and should understand with their heart" (v. 15). It is spiritual sight, spiritual hearing, and a spiritual heart transplant which Jesus is talking about. That is why Jesus concluded, "and should be converted, and I should heal [*iáomai*] them" (v. 15).

It was to open the way for this spiritual healing that Jesus died on the cross, taking upon Himself our punishment so that we might be saved (healed).

We must also keep in mind what we saw previously—there is an intimate connection between the components of man's nature. That is the reason we have psychosomatic illness. This intimate connection was referred to by our Lord on two occasions: when He healed the man at the pool of Bethesda (John 5:1–18) and when He healed the crippled man lowered down through the roof in Capernaum (Mark 2:1–12). In the first incident, Jesus warned the man, "Sin no more, lest a worse thing come unto thee" (John 5:14). It seems that this man probably suffered as a result of his own personal sin, since that is the clear implication of Jesus' words.

In the second incident, Jesus linked physical health and forgiveness of sin. He proved He could forgive sin by demonstrating that He could heal: "But that ye may know that the Son of man hath power on earth to forgive sins . . . I say unto thee, arise, and take up thy bed, and go thy way into thine house" (Mark 2:10–11). The spiritual comes first, then the physical. Our Lord's great concern is that no man remain in his sin.

Saved, and Yet to Be Saved

While spiritual healing is the primary emphasis in the atonement, we would not be fair to the biblical data to exclude physical healing. It is included in the atonement, but not for this present age. There is a sense in which we are now saved, but also a sense in which our salvation is yet to come.

Hebrews 9:28 says, "So Christ was once offered to bear the sins of many; and unto them that look for Him shall He appear the second time without sin unto salvation." So we are now saved, but yet to be saved.

A person might say that he is saved in both his spirit and his body. But while he could say that, he would be wrong. This is the result of failing to understand that there are two kinds of salvation.

Helping to clarify this for us is Romans 13:11, where Paul said, "knowing the time, that it is now high time to awake out of sleep: for now is our salvation nearer than when we believed." The word translated "time" is *kairós* (2540) and means an opportune time, a period of opportunity. It implies the necessity of the task at hand. Roman Christians were being persecuted by the Emperor Nero and many would die as a result. Their time was soon going to be up. Like Jesus, they were going to die at a particular time. There was to be no escape for them. Suffering was not going to be eliminated just because they were Christians; in fact, it nearly assured it.

So, for these Roman Christians they had already received one kind of salvation—spiritual. They were closer to the physical, bodily salvation than when they believed. That becomes a motivation for godly living during suffering.

Our bodies are now saved only insofar as they are kept by the Spirit. Someday, as Hebrews 9:28 says, the remainder of our salvation—the liberation of our bodies from all sickness—will happen.

10

Did Jesus Announce That He Came to Save, to Heal, or Both?

What was the real purpose or goal that Jesus demonstrated in His ministry?

A Significant Sabbath

One Sabbath day, we read in Luke 4:16–21, Jesus went to the synagogue and declared the intentions of His ministry. We see that it was "His custom" (v. 16) to attend the synagogue. He proceeded to read from the scroll of Isaiah. After reading from a portion of the prophet, Jesus said, "This day is this Scripture fulfilled in your ears" (v. 21).

Luke 4:18–19 records Jesus' words as He read from Isaiah 61:1–2: "The Spirit of the Lord is upon Me, because He hath anointed Me to preach the gospel to the poor; He hath sent Me to heal the brokenhearted, to preach deliverance to the captives, and recovering of sight to the blind, to set at liberty them that are bruised, to preach the acceptable year of the Lord."

How are we to interpret these conditions Jesus mentions? We noted in Matthew 8:17 that even though on the cross the Lord Jesus bore our weaknesses, we still become ill and sick at times. Then we looked at 1 Peter 2:24 and saw that the primary purpose of Jesus' coming was to deal with our spiritual sickness. We did this by going back to the Old Testament to see what the original passage taught. The passage there in Isaiah 53 referred primarily to our sin-sickness.

Coming now to Isaiah 61:1–2 from which our Lord read that day, Isaiah wrote, "the Lord has anointed Me to preach good tidings unto the meek." The quotation in Luke 4 says, "to preach the gospel to the poor." So, the "poor" are the "meek." That is what Jesus meant when He said, "Blessed are the poor in spirit: for theirs is the kingdom of heaven" (Matt. 5:3). These words are symbolic of something much more than financial or physical impoverishment.

The Lord continued in Isaiah, "He hath sent Me to bind up the brokenhearted." Did Jesus come to do heart surgery? Luke 4:18 says, "Heal the brokenhearted." So, this "healing" must be something greater than the literal variety.

Again, we find "to proclaim liberty to the captives." Remember that the political environment in Jesus' day was not freedom, but oppressive Roman occupation. Jesus, however, never preached rebellion against Rome. His enemies at His trial said, "We found this fellow perverting the nation, and forbidding to give tribute to Caesar, saying that He Himself is Christ, a king" (Luke 23:2). To this Jesus responded, "My kingdom is not of this world" (John 18:36).

The greatest interpreter of Jesus' theology was the apostle Paul. He wrote, "Servants, obey in all things your masters" (Col. 3:22). So, we cannot interpret "liberty to the captives" in a literal way. Jesus did not condone violence or rebellion against Rome.

And continuing in Isaiah, we read, "and recovery of sight to the blind." What "blindness" are we talking about? The context favors spiritual blindness as the primary emphasis.

It is interesting to note that Jesus did not fully quote Isaiah 61:2. He stopped at "to proclaim the acceptable year of the Lord." Christ did not come to earth the first time to execute judgment or God's justice. Jesus had told Nicodemus, "For God sent not His Son into the world to condemn the world; but that the world through Him might be saved" (John 3:17). If Jesus had quoted Isaiah 61:2 completely, some might get the wrong idea that judgment would come right after His ministry.

It was this delay in judgment that apparently confused John the Baptist, because we are told in Matthew 11:2–3: "Now when John had heard in prison the works of Christ, he sent two of his disciples, and said unto Him. Art thou He that should come, or do we look for another?"

One Little Word Makes a Difference

Frankly, there is not a single verse in the whole New Testament that teaches that Jesus Christ's coming into the world was primarily to heal the sick. Healing the sick can be (and has been) done by human beings, but forgiveness of sin is the unique prerogative of deity, and that is why the scribes reacted so strongly to Jesus' words when He announced to the crippled man who had been lowered through the roof, "Son, thy sins be forgiven thee" (Mark 2:5). One scribe correctly reasoned, ". . . who can forgive sin but God only?" (Mark 2:7).

Notice in Luke 4:18 that the King James Version uses italics to designate a word added to the translation. The New American Standard Version does this most of the time, but the New International Version does not use this procedure at all. What Jesus literally read is: "The Spirit of the Lord upon Me." There is no verb. The verb "is" (*eimí* [1510]) is not present. The same construction is found in Hebrew 13:8: "Jesus Christ the same yesterday, and today, and forever." Some modern translations insert "is" in italics (NASB) and some add it without italics (NIV).

What is the significance of this little word "is"? When the verb does not exist in the original Greek, it refers to an eternal relationship or character. In Hebrews 13:8, it is speaking of the character of Jesus Christ. He will always be loving to His people. He may permit sickness to come into one's life, but we should not interpret that to mean that Jesus suddenly loves us less. In fact, sickness or other major problems can actually indicate His great love for us, and their absence could indicate His displeasure (see Heb. 12:5–8).

Did you ever stop to think that through sickness God may accomplish a far greater work in your life or mine than if He granted us a continuous number of healthy years? Does not Paul say that about his "thorn" when he says, "Most gladly therefore, will I rather glory in my infirmities [*astheneíais* {769}], that the power of Christ may rest upon me" (2 Cor. 12:9)? We shun suffering, but it may contribute to the outworking of God's grand design and purpose—not only for us but for everyone in our sphere of influence.

In Luke 4:18, the absence of *eimí* (is) stresses the perfect agreement between the three Persons of the Trinity. There is a perfect symmetry of purpose between all the Persons of the Godhead. What one did, the others endorsed completely.

He Came to "Heal"

Jesus, when quoting Isaiah 61:1, said that "He hath sent Me to heal the broken hearted" (Luke 4:18). What kind of healing did He mean? We shall examine three Greek words that refer to healing:

Sṓzō (4882)

Sṓzō means to deliver from disease or demon possession (Matt. 9:21–22; Mark 3:4; 5:23, 28, 34; 6:56; 10:52; Luke 6:9; 8:36, 48, 50; 17:19; 18:42; John 11:12). Twenty times this verb refers to spiritual salvation (Matt. 1:21; 10:22; 19:25; 24:13, 22; Mark 8:35; 10:26; 13:13, 20; 16:16; Luke 7:50; 8:12; 9:24; 13:23; 18:26; 19:10; John 3:17; 5:34; 10:9; 12:47).

Sṓzō is also used in James 5:15. This "healing" actually brings the person to a position of dependence upon God. When someone is sick (note that it does happen to believers) the elders of the church are to be called upon. They are to "anoint" or rub oil on the sick (apply available medical means) and pray for him, "And the wish [*euchḗ* {2171}] of faith shall save the sick, and the Lord shall raise him up."

Therapeúō (2323)

This verb is used in Matthew 8:16: "When the even was come . . . He . . . healed all that were sick."

Therapeúō means to take care of the sick, to heal showing concern and compassion. It is related to *therápōn* (2324), attendant, servant.

Iáomai (2390)

This is the third Greek word used for "heal." When we examined 1 Peter 2:24, we saw that the phrase, "by whose stripes ye were healed," referred to spiritual healing—in other words, salvation. (See chapter 9 entitled, "What Did Jesus Cancel on the Cross?") We looked at the context of 1 Peter 2:24 and saw that the overwhelming evidence points to sin as the real sickness. In an earlier chapter we showed the connection between our spiritual lives and our physical lives. The Scriptures teach what modern medicine has now admitted—there is such a thing as psychosomatic illness.

We also took a look at Isaiah 53 from which Peter quotes and established that Isaiah's theme was primarily sin. Consequently, we concluded that both Isaiah and Peter were referring to healing in a spiritual sense.

This view is confirmed by 1 Peter 2:25 which says, "For ye were as sheep going astray; but are now returned unto the Shepherd and Bishop of your souls." The word "returned" is *epistréphō* (1994) and is translated "converted" in Matthew 13:15 which says, "lest at any time they . . . should be converted [*epistréphō*] and I heal [*iáomai*] them."

Iáomai is also used for physical healing. The story of the crippled man lowered through the roof (Luke 5:19–26) uses *iáomai* in verse 17 where it says, "and the power of the Lord was present to heal them."

We also noted that Matthew 8:17 gives us warrant for saying that physical healing was indeed included in the death of Jesus Christ. He did not fail in His work on the cross; it is merely a benefit that may be delayed until we have our resurrection bodies. We noted that our *apolútrōsis* (629), complete redemption, occurs later (Rom. 8:23).

The question then is, did Jesus mean physical or spiritual healing in Luke 4:18? The context is not literal, so the healing referred to here cannot be taken literally in its primary sense either. The physical healings were not Christ's primary purpose. He came, as the angel of the Lord said to Joseph, to "save His people from their sins" (Matt. 1:21).

The Only One Who Can Save

First Peter 2:24 clearly teaches that Jesus died a physical death on the cross. He did something physical which has a spiritual benefit that can be ours by faith. Just because He did something physical that benefits us spiritually does not mean that we can do the same.

There are many examples of this confused thinking, but two will suffice. There are some who rely solely on the physical act of their baptism and believe they are Christians because of it. There are some who cross themselves and believe that this act renders them holy. In itself, there is nothing wrong with either one, but the danger with both is that people can be easily deceived. No physical act, except Christ's life, death, and resurrection, can benefit us as far as our salvation is concerned.

Some biblical examples will prove this. In Luke 11:17–44, Jesus was criticized by some Pharisees because He had not washed His hands ceremonially before eating (v. 38). There is nothing wrong with washing one's hands, but it does not do a thing as far as our relationship to the Lord is concerned. Spiritual cleansing on the inside is the important thing, not external ceremonies (vv. 39–44).

Our understanding of spiritual things is upside down if we think that the common dirt of this world makes us unholy when it was the sin of man that caused the earth to be cursed (Gen. 3:17–18). Evidently Uzzah made this same mistake when he thought that the Ark of the Covenant would be defiled if it touched the ground, but not if he touched it (2 Sam. 6:6–7). Was not his touch a greater defilement, for his body was a sinful body as is ours?

So, we are called to faith in what Jesus Christ did for us. We are called to abandon all efforts at "doing" something to have peace with the Father (Rom. 9:16). Jesus is the only way. If you have not sought Jesus in faith, we urge you to do so today. Do not trust in anything you can do. He has already done it all.

11

Forgiveness of Sins and Healing

Luke 4:18 is a verse which is frequently quoted to support faith-healing. In the process, words are pressed into service to teach what the context does not teach. Words like "poor," "brokenhearted," and "deliverance" are used without reference to the overall ministry goals of the Lord Jesus Christ. This is especially true of the word "heal." Is God able to heal? Certainly, He is! Yet He chooses (and He alone makes such determinations) what He will or will not do. His ways are not always predictable, because He is sovereign.

We have seen that the context of a word must be considered to determine its meaning in each setting. We saw in 1 Peter 2:24 that *iáomai* (2390) can mean either physical or spiritual healing. It was the context of the word that showed us or gave us its meaning in that verse.

The Scriptures indicate that man is a captive to sin and Satan. That is why Paul wrote that unbelievers must repent, "that they may recover themselves out of the snare of the devil, who are taken captive by him at his will" (2 Tim. 2:26). Believers, then, are truly and actually liberated from sin, but this is spiritual liberation, not necessarily political liberation.

So, it is our responsibility to study this verse in great detail, examining every word in it and comparing other Scriptures to see how a word is used and applied.

The Pressing Need

Jesus said He came, "to preach the gospel." Why "preach the gospel" when there are so many other problems like political oppression, human rights violations, poverty, and so on? It is because in the greatest, most pressing need, humanity finds its answer in the gospel. It is our only and best hope.

Jesus came "to preach deliverance to the captives" (KJV). The New American Standard Version says, "Proclaim release to the captives," and the New International Version says, "freedom for the prisoners." The word "deliverance" is *áphesis* (859), and means forgiveness. Jesus came, He said, to provide a means or way of forgiveness.

The greatest captive of all is not the political prisoner; it is not the man behind prison bars. There are other captivities much worse than this. Consider a person who smokes. He knows it is killing him. He has heard the warnings and read it on the package, but he is a captive. It is the same with the alcoholic. They are slaves to their sinful habits. That is why taxes on tobacco and alcohol are called "sin" taxes. Sin is the greatest captivator of all.

Jesus said that He would "set at liberty them that are bruised." "To set at liberty" means to save. The purpose of Jesus in coming to the world was to save His people from their sins (Matt. 1:21).

We saw that the context of Luke 4:18 is found in Isaiah 61. When that portion was examined, we noted that its general tenor did not refer to political oppression nor to sickness, but to the captivity which sin has created. We also noted that Jesus did not quote Isaiah 61:2 in its entirety because He did not come to condemn but to "save His people from their sins." The bringing out of justice, the final accounting, has been delayed. He came to initiate the age of forgiveness.

The most important reassurance anyone can have is to be rescued from the powerful reign of sin in his life. That is why believers who have a serious, life-threatening illness often are not overly concerned about healing. The realization of their human frailty makes their eternal destiny and their relationship to God even more precious.

Here is where the graciousness of the Lord becomes more apparent. Paul speaks in Romans 2:4 of "the riches of His goodness and forbearance." When we have our health, we are enjoying the goodness of God. Few people, however, come to their senses during the "good times." It seems that sometimes we almost force God to send illness our way.

What is the most important thing we should pray for when we are sick? If we do not know the Lord, we should repent and pray for forgiveness. You see, the goodness of God is that He does the thing that is necessary that we might seek out the eternal issues.

He may put us on our backs so that we are forced to look up.

Mark 2:1–12 records the incident of a crippled man carried on his bed and lowered through the roof to be healed by Jesus. His friends cared about him. That is how our hearts should feel when we see the sick around us. This man's friends were persistent, insistent, and creative in getting their friend to Jesus. All involved in this incident had faith. Mark records that Jesus "saw their faith" (v. 5), and then He said, "Son, thy sins be forgiven thee." Faith here is presupposed. The word for "forgiveness" is *áphesis* which Jesus used in Luke 4:18. Actually, it is in the perfect tense—"have been forgiven." His sins had already been forgiven.

Of course, the scribes correctly reasoned, "Who can forgive sins but God only?" (v. 7). Jesus' response was a claim to His deity. Which is more important and which is easier—to heal the man or forgive his sins? Jesus showed He could do both. He gave them a sign which they could visibly see so that they might believe what they could not see. Some think that the important act here is the physical healing, but the all-important fact is that this man's sins were forgiven.

The Person of Christ

If Jesus came to preach healing, then He would not have healed people individual by individual. All He would have had to do was to speak the word and all the diseases and deformities on earth would have disappeared. Since He did not do that, that could not have been His primary mission. Many people received the benefit of physical healing but did not receive forgiveness of sins—yet many people today see physical healing as a greater miracle than the forgiveness of sins.

The word translated "preach the gospel" is *euaggelísasthai* (2097, MT), and is in the aorist middle infinitive. The aorist refers to the purpose of Christ's incarnation. Its present tense (*euaggelízesthai* [TR]) stresses the idea that it is a repeated or continual action. His life was one of telling the good news, for He wanted the world to know that there was forgiveness of sins. After His temptation by the devil in the wilderness, Jesus immediately began to preach. Matthew 4:17 says, "From that time on Jesus began to preach and say, Repent: for the kingdom of heaven is at hand."

Jesus preached of *Himself*. He said, "Come unto *Me*, all ye that labor and are heavy laden, and I will give you rest" (Matt. 11:28). Paul emphasized that the gospel message is the "Jesus Christ message" when he wrote, "For we preach not ourselves, but Christ Jesus the Lord" (2 Cor. 4:5). That is the same focus of Philip, one of the first deacons who "went down to the city of Samaria, and preached Christ to them" (Acts 8:5).

The word *euaggelízomai* is never used for healing. It is only used for preaching the gospel. First Timothy 1:15 says, "This is a faithful saying, and worthy of all acceptation, that Christ Jesus came into the world to save sinners." Did Paul say "to heal sinners"? No, that was not Jesus' primary mission.

The purpose of the miracles of Jesus was to point out to everyone who He really was. John wrote down the miracles of our Lord for a specific purpose. He said, "And many other signs truly did Jesus in the presence of His disciples, which are not written in this book: But these are written, that ye might believe that Jesus is the Christ, the Son of God; and that believing ye might have life through His name" (John 20:30–31).

The writer of Hebrews said, "And being made perfect He became the author of eternal salvation" (Heb. 5:9). The verb "to make perfect" is *teleióō* (5048) which means to have reached the goal for which He came. Jesus had a goal in mind, the goal that the Father had commissioned Him to accomplish. He reached that goal. On the cross He said, "It is finished" (John 19:30). That is the word *teleióō*. He, therefore, was the "author," the *aítios* (159), or the cause or reason for our salvation.

We must never forget that Jesus Christ is the center of the gospel because He is the gospel. He is the "root" of the gospel. We are the "fruit" of the gospel.

The Personal Response

When we compare the healing ministry of Jesus with His ministry of forgiveness, we notice that there is always a condition of faith placed on the latter, but that is not always the case with the former.

Jesus went about "preaching the gospel of the kingdom" (Matt. 4:23). This is the good news of a spiritual kingdom. The good news is that the Lord Jesus, who is not only the preacher but also the message preached, will establish His rule in our hearts and will cleanse us from all evil if we yield ourselves fully to Him. This requires personal faith in the Lord. He does not create a new body for us now, but He does save our souls.

Now, there are some people who say that if we are not healed, it is because we lack faith. That really cannot be sustained from Scripture. It is true that Jesus questioned people's faith in many instances, but not always. Matthew 4:23 tells us that Jesus was "healing all manner of sickness and all manner of disease among the people." He did this irrespective of what diseases they had and irrespective of whether they had faith or not. They were healed because they were there.

The same cannot be said about forgiveness. When the Lord Jesus was crucified, two thieves were also crucified with him. One repented, and the other did not (Luke 23:39–43). The Lord forgave only the one who repented.

You see, physical healing and spiritual healing are not on the same level. Some preachers are confusing people because they do not recognize this difference. Their message is that all believers ought to be healed.

As we have seen, healing was indiscriminate when Jesus healed the multitudes, but forgiveness of sins was always personal and individual. When we examined Matthew 1:21, we noted that it does not say that Jesus came to heal. Jesus came, as John the Baptist said, as the "lamb of God, which taketh away the sin of the world."

Mary was told by the angel, "He shall be great, and shall be called the Son of the Highest" (Luke 1:32). There was no mention of His suffering and death. The angel continued, "and the Lord God shall give to Him the throne of His father David" (v. 32). We have the beginning and ending of Jesus' ministry, but there is no mention of a healing ministry being established.

What we are not hearing from the faith healers today is that healing for Jesus, although flowing from His compassion for people, was far less important than people consider it to be today. Our Lord's great passion was for the souls of mankind.

Another important difference between healing and forgiveness is that others besides the Lord Jesus can bring healing to physical problems, but only the Lord Jesus can forgive sins. That is why Peter said, "There is no other name under heaven given among men, whereby we must be saved" (Acts 4:12).

Healing can be counterfeited. We cannot necessarily assume that if something is supernatural, it comes from God. Scripture warns us about the Antichrist. The prefix "anti" means either "in lieu of" or "against." Revelation 13:13–14 describes his action which includes "great wonders" (v. 13) with the result that he "deceives them that dwell on the earth by means of those miracles which he had power to do" (v. 14). You see, it is possible to do miracles (*sēmeía* [4592]) and yet be an antichrist.

There are reports of healings in pagan religions all over the world—of arms being lengthened and eyes opened. There are fakes and real wonder-workers out there who are not saved. Jesus did not say that a person had to be a believer to heal. "Many will say to Me in that day, Lord, Lord, have we not prophesied in Thy name? and in Thy name have cast out devils? and in Thy name done many wonderful works? And then will I profess unto them, I never knew you" (Matt. 7:22–23).

So a Christian should be wary because he knows these things can happen. We must ask if ministries which place undue stress on physical healing are following our Lord's procedure or is it being done "for filthy lucre's sake" (Titus 1:11)? Just because a person holds a Bible in his hand and performs a healing does not mean that he is a prophet of God.

The Permanent Benefit

Earlier we looked at Hebrews 5:9 where it says, "He became the author of eternal salvation unto all them that obey Him." Because this "Author" is eternal, the salvation He brings is eternal, too. Our hope is placed squarely on the Person of the Lord Jesus Christ. Remember, He never changes (Heb. 13:8).

When a person becomes a believer, he receives an eternal salvation. When a person is healed, he receives a temporary healing. You see, everything in this world, except God's word, is temporary. Someone has rightly said, "Lazarus had one cradle but two graves." So, the lesser of the two benefits is physical healing. Others besides Jesus (even unbelievers) can heal people, but only Jesus can forgive, and His forgiveness is permanent. That is why we urge you to focus on the real problem. You could be physically healthy but spiritually sick.

The Postponed Healing

Recall the words of Romans 8:23: "We ourselves groan within ourselves, waiting for the adoption, to wit, the redemption of our body." The redemption (*apolútrōsis* [629]) of our bodies has not come yet. This is part of the Christians' hope. We know that we have been given the down payment of our salvation, and we eagerly await the rest.

The healing we see today may be of God, and certainly He can do it because He is sovereign, but much of it does not have His mark on it.

12

What Really Is the "Good News" That Jesus Preached?

Historically, "liberation theologies" have restricted words like "poor" to physical poverty, thereby reducing Jesus' mission to meeting physical needs. In this camp, some have sanctioned even revolution to make sure everyone gets adequate food, water, and medicine. More moderate views in the church have been placed under an umbrella called the "social gospel." Like faith-healing theologians, those who hold such views universalize imperatives since, they say, Jesus came to free *all* men from *all* political oppression as well as from all physical sickness.

But Jesus came "to preach the gospel." The word is *euaggelízomai* (2097). He came, as the middle voice indicates, to preach about Himself. In light of these controversial theologies, it is important to understand exactly what this entails.

"To the Poor"

We customarily regard poverty as a terrible curse, but this may not necessarily be the case. Paul wrote in 2 Corinthians 12:9, "Most gladly therefore will I rather glory in my infirmities, that the power of Christ may rest upon me."

When a person is physically weak, as we saw in a previous study, they are often more open to the ways of God. The same is true of the financially weak. The poor are forced to trust God because they must live by faith from day to day. It is not necessary, so people think, to pray for "our daily bread" (Matt. 6:11) when the pantry is full and the need for a diet is evident. The Lord Himself said that the rich were more complacent and self-sufficient. He stressed this when He said, "Children, how hard is it for them that trust in riches to enter into the kingdom of God. It is easier for a camel to go through the eye of a needle, than for a rich man to enter into the kingdom of God" (Mark 10:24–25). James' epistle brings out the same idea where he wrote: "Has not God chosen the poor of this world rich in faith? . . . Do not rich men oppress you, and draw you before the judgment seats?" (James 2:5–6).

God, of course, can do the difficult and save the rich (Mark 10:27). If you notice that when Paul wrote, "not many wise after the flesh, not many mighty, not many noble, are called" (1 Cor. 1:26), he did not say "not *any*" but "not *many.*" That is why AMG International uses newspaper evangelism to reach the literate, educated public in nations such as India and Indonesia. Thank the Lord that some of them, too, are captured in the net of the gospel.

So the poor here means physically poor, but it means something more, too. It means the humble, the spiritually impoverished ones. That "poor" is the kind referred to in Matthew 5:3, "Blessed are the poor in spirit." The word is *ptōchós* (4434) and means those who are helpless in their spirit. Not those who are helpless merely because of the unjust actions of others, but those who have realized their spiritual bankruptcy. They no longer blame God for their condition, but they say, I brought myself here, but come, Lord, and help me out of this. It is surrendering to God that same monster of human pride and self-sufficiency that led our original parents, Adam and Eve, to rebel. This is a real miracle in the human heart.

"He Has Sent Me"

There was a purpose for Jesus to come into this world. He came to do His Father's will. Remember Luke 4:18 said, "The Spirit of the Lord is upon Me." So, we see that the Holy Spirit certified Jesus as the Son of God. The Spirit was in complete harmony with the Son.

Now Jesus says, "He has sent Me." Here Jesus refers to the Father thus announcing that the work of the Messiah was not an individual act to be accomplished on His own. There is no selfishness in the Trinity.

The word used for "sent" is *apostéllō* (649) which comes from *apó* (575), from; and *stéllō* (4724), to send. There is another word, *pémpō* (3992), which implies a more random "sending." *Pémpō* is less directed, less purposeful than *apostéllō. Apostéllō* emphasizes the authority of the person who does the sending and the representative nature of the one who is sent. So without doubt, Jesus came with the full authorization of the Father. Paul used this same word when he wrote, "And how shall they preach except they be sent?" (Rom. 10:15).

The Lord Jesus Christ came for the specific goal of meeting mankind's greatest need which, as we have previously seen, is not temporary healing. If, when we minister, we heal the sick and feed the hungry, but have not preached the gospel, what good is that? All we may have done is to help a person live longer in order to sin more and bring more condemnation upon himself. We could actually be helping a child live to become a criminal.

This mission from the Father was first promised in Genesis 3:15. It is called the *protoeuaggélion* (the first gospel): ". . . and I will put enmity between you and the woman, and between your seed and her seed; it shall bruise your head, and you shall bruise his heel."

If you recall, in one of our Lord's parables He said, "The kingdom of heaven is like a treasure hid in a field, the which when a man has found, he hides, and for joy thereof goes and sells all that he has, and buys that field" (Matt. 13:44). There are no financial advantages that could possibly approach, equal, or surpass the freedom of being forgiven. That is why it is the Pearl of Great Price.

"To Heal the Brokenhearted"

What does this phrase mean? Does it mean to heal physically? The word is *iáomai* (2390)—which we examined in chapter two—and it is in the aorist tense.

This emphasizes that Jesus Christ was and is the means of its accomplishment.

When we looked at *iáomai* earlier, we noted that it was different than *therapéuō* (2323), which means to minister or to provide therapy. Even before that, though, we noted the constituent parts of man—his spirit, soul, and body. When the Father sent His Son into the world, He sent Him to deal with the total human personality. There are two major relationships: the horizontal dealing with our social relationships, and the vertical dealing with our spiritual relationship. Man tends to focus on the former and ignore the latter, but the spiritual relationship is, in reality, man's primary need.

It is the Father's plan to bring immediate justification and progressive sanctification, even though the believer remains in a corruptible body. There is a dynamic tension between eternity within us and the temporary around us. That is why Paul wrote, "And if children, then heirs; heirs of God, and joint-heirs with Christ; if it so be that we suffer with Him, that we may also be glorified together" (Rom. 8:17). The words "suffer with" are from one Greek word, *sumpáschō* (4841), from *sún* (4862), with; and *páschō* (3958), to suffer. We have Christ within us as we suffer here in this world.

It is vitally important that we realize that we can praise God even in our weaknesses and sufferings. In fact, this is often a far more powerful witness than any preacher can deliver, for it takes the grace of God to rejoice in our sufferings. Sometimes the only "gospel" anyone reads is the one they see in God's children. Paul wrote in 2 Corinthians 3:2, "You are our epistle written in our hearts, known and read of all men."

Remember, we also looked at *iáomai* in Matthew 13:15. In that verse there are many words which, if literally taken, would distort the mission of our Lord Jesus Christ. In the context, Jesus has just explained why He spoke in parables. When using words like "heart is waxed gross," He did not mean a fat heart or heart disease, and "dull of hearing" and "closed eyes" did not mean that they needed hearing aids or eye surgery. These are metaphors of deeper spiritual realities to which many people are insensitive. Without doubt, the "healing" in Matthew 13:15 must refer to spiritual healing.

Now, what does the word "brokenhearted" mean? The Greek word is *suntríbō* (4937) and comes from *sún,* with; and *tríbō* (n.f.), to break, to rub. Life has rubbed them wrong, has broken them down.

It is also noteworthy that the word *suntríbō* is in the middle voice, meaning that they have brought themselves into their current situation. It is not God's fault; it is their own responsibility. When a person reaches the point of recognizing this, he seeks for help and is thus in a position to become blessed. That is why the words of Matthew 5:3 are important to note: "Blessed are the poor in spirit: for theirs is the kingdom of heaven."

The verb *eimí* (1510), "is" or "to be," in this verse, is in the present active form. It is not a promise of a future blessing, not a will be, but is, right now in the present. There is an immediate blessing in coming to this point. We now are in the kingdom of heaven. That is why Paul wrote, "Who has delivered us from the power of darkness, and has translated us into the kingdom of His dear Son" (Col. 1:13).

What is amazing is that in God's way of dealing with us, He allows sin to "rub" us until we are broken in our hearts. When we see what we really are, we cry out for help. We are like Isaiah who said, "Woe is me! for I am undone; because I am a man of unclean lips, and I dwell in the midst of people of unclean lips: for my eyes have seen the King, the Lord of hosts" (Is. 6:5).

Someone has said that if you want to be discouraged, look inside; if you want to be depressed look around you; and if you want to be blessed, look upward. There is escape with the upward look. If you have not done that, we urge you to do so today.

"To Preach Deliverance to the Captives"

Here's another example of how a passage could be misunderstood. Some behind bars in our prisons could say that the Lord Jesus came to literally set them free. They could say, Well, I claim the promises of this verse for myself; I claim a release from my captivity. But the real question is this—is this promise to be taken physically or spiritually? The truth is that a person can be freer inside prison than those who are outside and are prisoners of sin. Many people are slaves to their own drives, the world's material goods, and the devil himself.

Again we must examine, we must observe, before we jump to conclusions and make incorrect applications of Scripture. The word "deliverance" is *áphesis* (859). It is the word used for forgiveness and it means "to loose." It comes from *apó,* from; and *híēmi* (n.f.), to send.

Forgiveness, you see, is the ability that only God has to lift off our sin and take it away from us. He detaches it from us and keeps us from it. Now as we look at sin, we hate it and want to flee from it. Even though sin still pursues us, we run from it. Instead of us chasing after sin, sin chases us. Because sin is no longer ruling over us, we are no longer seen or regarded by the Lord as guilty.

But could Luke 4:18 possibly apply to political captives? Jesus lived in Palestine, and His nation did not have its liberty. Rome was the occupying conqueror and collected the hated taxes. The Jews were looking for a Messiah who would free them from Rome. What did Jesus think of these political goals? John records an interesting event after Jesus had fed the five thousand: "When Jesus therefore perceived that they would come and take Him by force, to make Him a king, He departed again into a mountain Himself alone" (John 6:15). The people were excited with the thought that this man fed them all they wanted at no charge, and they decided He would make a good king. However, Jesus did not want anything to do with it. He went away into a mountain all by Himself.

Jesus did not become the kind of liberator that the Jews expected. That is one reason the cross is such an offense to the Jews. It appears to be a symbol of defeat and failure. And so Paul wrote, "We preach Christ crucified, unto the Jews a stumbling block, and unto the Greeks foolishness" (1 Cor. 1:23). The cross went against Jewish expectation. The King James Version, as in the Greek text, correctly puts "Christ" next to "crucified." To the Jewish mind, this was offensive, an impossible contradiction.

Could Jesus have overthrown Rome? Certainly He could have, but He did not because that was not His Father's plan, His plan, or the Holy Spirit's plan. For Jesus, political power was a "devilish" temptation, for had not the devil tempted Him earlier with the kingdoms of the whole world (Matt. 4:8–9)? And what was Christ's response? "Get thee hence, Satan: for it is written, you shall worship the Lord your God, and Him only shall you serve" (Matt. 4:10).

The word for "captives" in Luke 4:18 is *aichmalṓtois* (164). This is related to *aichmḗ* (n.f.), which is the tip of a sword. A soldier is captured and forced into surrender by the tip of the enemy's sword. The whole human race was taken captive by Satan, and the Lord's mission was to rescue His people (Matt. 1:21). When Jesus was accused of being empowered by Satan, He said, "How can one enter into a strong man's house, and spoil his goods, except he first bind the strong man?" (Matt. 12:29).

So, we emphasize the good news that the Lord Jesus Christ came to set us free from the guilt and the power of sin. He is our Rescuer.

"The Recovering of Sight to the Blind"

The Bible teaches that there are two kinds of blindness: physical and spiritual. The first is a temporary tragedy, but the latter is an eternal disaster. The Greek word translated "recovering of sight" is *anáblepsis* (309), and it is found only in Luke 4:18. It is from *aná* (303), again; and *blépō* (991), see, beware, take heed.

The healing of the blind man in John 9 could not be an *anáblepsis* since he had never had physical sight before Jesus healed him. How does this affect our understanding, and how can it be said that Jesus restores us so that we see again?

When humanity was created, it had the spiritual eyesight it lacks today. When Adam fell, he destroyed his spiritual eyes and became spiritually blind. He never again saw himself, his wife, or his Creator in the same way as he did before he fell. He saw his nakedness, he blamed his wife, and he fled from his Maker. That is why Jesus said to Nicodemus, "Except a man be born-again, he cannot see the kingdom of God" (John 3:3).

Darkness (*skótos* [4655]) is often used in the New Testament as a symbol for sin. Paul wrote, "Who has delivered us from the power of darkness" (Col. 1:13). "Darkness," however, in John 12:46 in the phrase, "that whosoever believeth on Me should not abide in darkness," is *skotía* (4653) which means the consequence of sin (cf. 1 John 1:5). Man was created to know God. He lost his ability to fellowship with God as a result of Adam's fall. Our Lord Jesus Christ came to restore man's spirit (his spiritual eyes), and He calls out to men and women today for this kind of healing.

"To Set at Liberty Them That Are Bruised"

Here Jesus again defines His ministry. The word translated "bruised" is the perfect passive participle of *thraúō* (2352). It refers to those who have been crushed by cruel oppressors. Is it not very cruel for Satan to hold people in spiritual captivity? It is cruel to hurt people even if only in their earthly life, but how much more cruel it is to draw people away to an eternal hell. Is it not cruel for Satan to tempt people into all kinds of life-damaging addictions? That is why we are to pray, "if God peradventure will give them repentance to the acknowledging of the truth; and that they may recover themselves out of the snare of the devil, who are taken captive by him at his will" (2 Tim. 2:25–26).

This phrase in Greek literally reads, "To send away crushed ones in deliverance." The word is *áphesis.* In this phrase it is preceded by the word en (1722) which means "in." Jesus said He would put these "crushed ones" in deliverance. He does not send us away wondering about our forgiveness. That is why He said, "All that the Father gives Me shall come to Me; and him that comes to Me I will in no wise cast out" (John 6:37).

The word translated "to send away" is *apostéllō.* Jesus is stressing His authority to grant this kind of forgiveness in full agreement and concordance with the Father and the Spirit. The aorist tense of this word stresses that Jesus is the means of the deliverance.

But not only are our sins "sent away," after we are rescued, Christ "sends us" into the world as witnesses.

13

Why Did Jesus Heal?

As we explained earlier, the key to understanding the Scripture is first to carefully observe the context of each verse; second is to interpret the verse, and third is to make an application of the verse. A careful observation of Luke 4 shows that the Lord Jesus did not come to earth to have people regard Him as merely a healer. He came here for a very specific purpose, and repeatedly He said that He came to preach the gospel, with Himself consciously the center of the message.

Jesus, though, did anticipate that people would tend to regard Him as a physician. He said that the people of Galilee would say to Him, "Physician, heal Thyself" (Luke 4:23). Yet, He called Himself a prophet when He said, "No prophet is accepted in his own country" (Luke 4:24).

This is illustrated perfectly when, after crowds gathered because of His healing, He left for other towns saying, "Let us go into the next towns, that I may preach there also: for therewith came I forth" (Mark 1:38). In fact, Mark's gospel (1:1) starts off with the Christ-centeredness of the gospel when He said, as the New International Version translates it, "The beginning of the gospel about Jesus Christ, the Son of God." He is the message because the gospel centers on Him.

Jesus' message was "to preach the acceptable year of the Lord" (Luke 4:19). He preached that the people were to accept Him and His reign in their hearts. Jesus' primary purpose, you see, was not to heal people physically. That was merely an incidental element to His main purpose of preaching. The healing ministry He demonstrated was first of all a verification of who He was, but it was not His primary purpose.

"He Was Moved with Compassion" (Matt. 9:36)

One of the reasons Jesus healed was His compassion for people. The noun "compassion" is an excellent English word that translates the verb *splagchnízomai* (4697). The *splágchna* (4698) are the inner organs of a person which, the Greeks thought, were the location of the human emotions. It is what we mean when we say we are "stirred up." The English word "compassion" comes from the Latin word *cum,* meaning "with" as in "cumulate," and the Greek word *páschō* (3958), which means to bear or suffer as in the word "pathos" (*páthos* [3806], inner passion).

Jesus healed because He had deep feelings for the human race. He cares because He was fully human (Heb. 4:15). He knew what it felt like to be healthy, and so He restored health to others. He knew hunger and gave crowds of people food when they had gone without to hear Him preach.

When the two blind men came to Him and cried out for mercy (Matt. 20:30), it says that "Jesus had compassion on them and touched their eyes" (v. 34). Similarly, when He fed the five thousand (Matt. 14:15–21) and the four thousand (Matt. 15:32–39), it specifically states that He had compassion on the people. He said, "I will not send them away fasting, lest they faint in the way."

We as believers are to have the same compassion. First John 3:17 says, "But whoso has this world's good, and sees his brother have need, and shuts up his bowels of compassion from him, how dwells the love of God in him?" There is an intimate connection between the love (*agápē* [26]) of God and the compassion (*splágchna*) of God. These are essentially synonymous words. To have love is to have compassion.

When John recorded "for God so loved the world" in John 3:16, we could replace "loved" with "had compassion." He knew mankind's greatest need as well as his lesser needs. We, of course, tend to see our physical needs as more important than our spiritual needs, and so we are prone to hear "heal" in a too-literal sense. This tendency showed itself when the disciples were told to "Beware of the leaven of the Pharisees" and understood it to mean that they should buy bread (Mark 8:15–16).

We know that we have a compassionate Lord Jesus Christ sent to us out of concern for our lost condition. We know that Jesus healed out of His compassionate heart.

"Have Mercy on Me, O Lord" (Matt. 15:22)

Many today are preaching that there is a sense in which God owes us healing. It is not phrased that bluntly, but the idea is there. It is often masked by a simile or Scripture and is quoted in a certain way, but it is a demand on God nonetheless.

That demanding spirit is nothing new to the human race. The Israelites succumbed to this in the wilderness. In Psalm 78:18 it says, "And they tempted God in their heart by asking meat for their lust." The word "asking" is the Hebrew word *sha al* (7592, OT) and the context in Psalm 78 indicates it was not merely a request, but a demand. The New International Version translates it, "They willfully put God to the test by demanding the food they craved." This verse refers back to the incident in Numbers 11 and the demands of the disgruntled for more variety in their diet. A demanding spirit shows that we are only concerned with the present and not so concerned about God's long-term viewpoint.

When people came to Jesus to be healed, they did not demand it or "claim" it. They asked for mercy. The Canaanite woman cried out, "Have mercy on me, O Lord" (Matt. 15:22). The word for "mercy" is *éleos* (1656). Bartimeaus also begged for mercy when he said, "Jesus, Thou Son of David, have mercy on me" (Mark 10:47).

Now, there are two words that are often used together: mercy and grace. Grace is the word *cháris* (5485), and it carries a different meaning than *éleos* or mercy. *Cháris* is the supernatural action of God in a human being that removes sin and enables a person to resist it. It is the element of change in a human being. *Éleos* is the expression of concern, compassion for the results of sin, either from the perspective of all of humanity or for the individual. A human cannot exercise grace, but he can exhibit mercy. Only the Lord can grant grace.

When the Lord Jesus came, He was "full of grace and truth" (John 1:14), and He showed mercy as a result. An important point to keep in mind is that grace always changes an individual's relationship to the Lord and to sin, but the Lord does not always change the consequences of sin in a person's life.

If a person has been a heavy drinker, God can give victory over this sin. He may, in fact, even heal that person's damaged liver, too. He gives grace to conquer the sin, but He may not grant the mercy to counteract its consequences. We cannot demand mercy. If you think about it, mercy is a pure gift just as grace is. A gift cannot be forced or pried from the giver's hand, because then it would no longer be a gift. The Lord is not accountable to our demands.

"Therefore He Has Mercy on Whom He Will" (Rom. 9:18)

So mercy cannot be forced by us on our side of the equation. The question is, then, do the Scriptures indicate whose decision it is? Logic alone would tell us that if it is not our right to demand, then the decision must rest in the Lord's hand.

Romans 9:18 says, "Therefore has He mercy on whom He will have mercy, and whom He will He hardens." Superficially, this refers to whomever God wants to give or grant mercy. Healing is one aspect of the mercy of God, but it is not an obligation on His part. All we can do is ask, not demand.

The prayer of faith referred to in James 5:15 is actually the word *euchē* (2171), and it is better translated as "wish" or "vow." When we pray for healing, we must not come with a demanding spirit. We must humbly acknowledge that God knows best. We know what our will for ourselves is—we want health. What we do not know is God's will (Eph. 1:9). If God wanted to heal everybody, He could, of course, do it with a mere word from His mouth.

The Greek word for "will" is *thélēma* (2307). What God wills, He has the definite ability to perform. It is the Lord's sovereign will which decides who will be healed and who will not.

So, we must be careful not to pray one thing and then say something else. We pray, "Thy will be done in earth, as it is in heaven" (Matt. 6:10). How can we pray for His will to be done and then turn around and demand that our particular will be carried out? Even Jesus ended His prayer by saying, "Thy will be done" (Luke 22:42; John 5:30).

Paul continues discussing God's will when He says, "What if God, willing to show His wrath, and to make His power known, endured with much longsuffering the vessels of wrath fitted for destruction?" (Rom. 9:22). The words "fitted for destruction" are one Greek word, *katartízō* (2675). The *Hebrew-Greek Key Study Bible* shows that it is in the passive voice. Now, what does this mean? If God directly hardens hearts by some action on His part, then He is the direct cause of sin and rebellion, and we know this is not the case for the holy God.

If we examine the situation of Pharaoh, we get some hints as to the answer of this seeming contradiction. In Exodus 7:3 God says, "And I will harden Pharaoh's heart," and just ten verses later it says, "And He hardened Pharaoh's heart" (v. 13). Yet in Exodus 8:15 it says, "But when Pharaoh saw there was a respite, he hardened his heart." The same sun that melts the wax hardens the clay.

This process of how both can be true at once is fully described in Romans 1:24–28. Here Paul uses the word *paradídōmi* (3860) three times, which the King James Version translates as "God gave them up" (vv. 24, 26) or "God gave them over" (v. 28). All that the Lord needs to "do" to harden a man's or a woman's heart is to "do" nothing at all to counteract sin's hardening effect on the human heart. All He needs to do is to let sin run its course. When we examine how the sins listed in Romans 1 get more and more heinous, then we see what *paradídōmi* really means.

The Lord acts according to His sovereign will. He permits us to be sick or mistreated or persecuted for our greater long-term good. That is why Joseph could say to his apprehensive brothers, "But as for you, you thought evil against me" (Gen. 50:20). Joseph in no way minimized his brothers' sinful actions of selling him and lying to his father. Yet, he went on to say, "but God meant it unto good, to bring to pass, as it is this day, to save much people alive" (Gen. 50:20).

So, if we are believers, we must come to that point of a humble, personal maturity of patiently waiting for the Lord's timing during our problems. We must learn to become obedient children and not grumble or demand.

"They That Are Whole Need Not a Physician" (Matt. 9:12)

There is a teaching among us today that Jesus was anti-physician. It is true that Luke is the only doctor mentioned by name, but he is referred to by Paul the apostle as "the beloved physician" (Col. 4:14). So, it is obvious that Paul was not opposed to physicians nor had he a "Who needs a doctor as long as we have Jesus?" attitude.

Jesus Himself said that "They that are whole need not a physician, but they that are sick" (Matt. 9:12). He saw Himself as a spiritual physician. The context, if we observe closely, is that He had just called the tax-collector Matthew (v. 9) and had eaten with some despised sinners (v. 10). He knew that we often forget that sin is the worst sickness that a person could possibly have.

If you remember the incident of the woman who had a twelve-year problem with bleeding, you will notice how Mark records the event: "and had suffered many things of many physicians" (Mark 5:26). So there were enough doctors, but they just did not have the necessary skill to help her.

The Good Samaritan Parable (Luke 10:25–37) shows us an important practical principle. Don't you think that the good Samaritan would have taken the man to an emergency room if there had been one available? Certainly, he would have, because he had compassion (Luke 10:33). He took him to the best place that was available to rest and recuperate and used what medicinal means he had. That is what we are to do, too.

We are never to ignore prayer to the Lord when we are sick; we are never to reject the supernatural. But just because we believe in the supernatural does not mean that it is more "spiritual" if we reject the natural, God-given medicinal means at our disposal.

All physicians, whether they realize it or not, depend on the supernatural. Doctors need to recognize their limitations and we need to gratefully accept the benefit they bring.

"He Shall Have Judgment without Mercy" (James 2:13)

Jesus said that He came "to preach the acceptable year of the Lord" (Luke 4:19). The word "acceptable" is *dektós* (1184) and means to accept or decide favorably. Now is the time when God extends His mercy and grace. Will there be a time to come when mercy, grace, and favor will not be available? This is implied in Jesus' words.

The story of the rich man and Lazarus gives some additional insight. The rich man begged for mercy. Luke 16:24 says, "And he cried and said, Father Abraham, have mercy on me, and send Lazarus, that he may dip the tip of his finger in water, and cool my tongue." Notice that he asked only temporary relief for himself. His focus was still on himself and the immediate. He was really the same person in Hades as he was on earth. His greatest problem was sin, but no mercy was possible for him then. His "acceptable" time was past. That is why Paul wrote, "Now is the accepted time; behold, now is the day of salvation" (2 Cor. 6:2). So, unless a person turns to God in faith before death, there is no mercy available afterwards.

In James 2:13 it says, "For he shall have judgment without mercy." The words "without mercy" are one Greek word, *anéleos* (MT, UBS, Nestle's Text; *aníleōs* [448] in the TR) which is the negative form of the word for "mercy" (*éleos*). So for some people there will be no mercy at the judgment. James goes on to identify this group as those "that have showed no mercy."

James has taken us to the afterlife, much like Jesus did in Luke 16. Did the rich man show mercy to poor Lazarus while he lived on earth? No, not at all. This is an eternal principle—our heart attitude toward others reveals whether God has really changed us. Having received mercy, we value it highly.

Our Lord taught this same principle in His parable of the unmerciful servant in Matthew 18:21–35. The servant was forgiven a huge debt, but he then turned to a fellow servant who owed him considerably less and refused to forgive the debt. The master said to the unmerciful servant, "Should not you also have had compassion on your fellowservant, even as I had pity on you?" (v. 33). Then the unmerciful servant was taken away to be punished.

So it might appear that two groups who will not be shown mercy at the judgment are those who are not born-again and those who will not show mercy to others. But this would be a wrong conclusion. These are not two groups, but two descriptions of the same group. That is why John wrote, "But whoso has this world's good, and sees his brother have need, and shuts up his bowels of compassion from him, how dwells the love of God in him?" (1 John 3:17).

The Lord is clearly telling us that when we have received mercy, it makes us a channel of blessing to others. We have the love of God graciously given to us, and so we are to let it overflow to others. If we are not merciful, we should examine our hearts to see if God's mercy has been received by us. Remember that Jesus said, "Blessed are the merciful: for they shall obtain mercy" (Matt. 5:7; see author's study, *The Beatitudes: The Pursuit of Happiness.)*

We have all done and said things that we cannot undo. We cannot retract our past sinful actions. We can only plead for mercy for ourselves and grant mercy to those who have hurt us.

"And All . . . Wondered at His Gracious Words" (Luke 4:22)

When Jesus finished reading the Scripture from Isaiah, "The eyes of all them that were in the synagogue were fastened on Him" (Luke 4:20). The crowd was amazed at what Jesus was telling them. Then Jesus astounded them further by saying, "This day is this Scripture fulfilled in your ears" (Luke 4:21).

Luke records that they all "wondered at the gracious words which proceeded from His mouth" (v. 22). Literally it reads, "the words of grace." In the next verse, Jesus knew that the crowds would misinterpret His real mission because He said, "You will surely say unto Me this proverb, Physician, heal yourself" (v. 23).

Thus Christ's mission was to be one of dispensing grace to people. He knew, though, that when people heard His words they would focus on the physical healings. He knew that the crowd in the synagogue was hoping for miracles because He said that they wanted "Whatsoever we have heard done in Capernaum, do also here in Your country" (v. 23).

But Jesus' emphasis was not on healing but speaking—even though He knew that "No prophet is accepted in his own country" (v. 24). The word for "accepted" is *dektón,* as also in verse 19. The irony here is clear: Jesus came to announce God's favor toward people and His own hometown did not favor Him!

Then, to press the point that God's mercy is unearned and selective, Jesus pointed to two clear Old Testament examples of God working with Gentiles instead of Jews. He cited Elijah's help of a widow in Phoenicia (vv. 25, 26) and Elisha's healing of a Syrian leper (v. 27). These two examples show the true nature of mercy, for it cannot be earned nor can it be demanded.

How unlike Jesus modern faith healers are! They imply that healing is a right we are to exercise instead of an uncoerced, merciful act of the Lord. They overwhelmingly emphasize the here-and-now and not the eternal. Man is made sovereign, as if he knows what is best and the Lord is woefully ignorant. There is a focus on the financial costs whereas Jesus healed without cost.

What is the cause of this? It is due to a failure to observe the context, interpret the words properly, and apply the Scriptures accurately.

14

What Were Jesus' Healing Methods?

There are people today who imagine that they are duplicating Jesus' healing ministry because they are mimicking His methods, but when we observe Jesus' methods of healing, we see that He certainly was neither uniform nor consistent in His procedures. Earlier we noted that He sometimes healed people who had shown faith, and at other times He healed crowds of people where faith was not a requirement. We are also going to see that sometimes His methods would not be acceptable today, nor would faith healers attempt to use such unusual methods.

The Lord Does Not Change, but His Methods Do

There are some who look at how Jesus or the apostle Paul did something and say, This is it! This is the method we must follow! However, if we carefully observe, interpret, and then apply, we will find that even though the Lord does not change, His mode of action often does. He adapts His power to the circumstances that exist, and the person who sees God's hand behind every circumstance stops being enslaved by the situation and is guided by the Lord through the problem.

A good example of this is God's dealings with the Israelites. He called them out of Egypt, led them in their wilderness travels for forty years, and fed them with manna from heaven. But why? Simply because there was no way for them to cultivate land as they wandered in the desert.

Does that mean that we are to quit our jobs and wait for manna out of heaven? In fact, if we did, we would be violating Paul's clear command, "This we commanded you, that if anyone would not work, neither should he eat" (2 Thess. 3:10).

We cannot stand over our gardens and claim power to produce fruit and vegetables without effort on our part, nor can we just quit our jobs. We cannot despise the normal means available to meet our needs. After all, even a tree's fruit needs to be picked. And even Jesus' mother labored in pain before His birth, which was preceded by a normal nine-month gestation period.

No More Manna

As the Jews entered the promised land, something happened to their automatic food supply. It stopped. In Joshua 5:12 it says, "And the manna ceased on the morrow after they had eaten of the old corn of the land; neither had the children of Israel manna any more." Did God change? No, of course not, but how He dealt with the people's need for food did change.

If anybody tells you that God will do today what He did before, refer them to Joshua 5:12.

Can you imagine some people's reaction? Why did the manna stop? Where's the manna?! Doesn't God love us anymore?

God wanted to teach the Israelites a lesson: what He does for the people today, He may not do the same way tomorrow. Notice that the Lord did not even wait twenty-four hours for the manna to elapse.

We must observe carefully, interpret, then apply. As we noted in an earlier portion, "Jesus Christ, the same yesterday, and today, and forever" (Heb. 13:8) refers to His nature, not His dealings with human beings. We cannot assume that because Moses parted the Red Sea, we can too.

Sometimes He Blesses (*Eulogéō*)

When our Lord Jesus blesses something, what does He do? The word "bless" is *eulogéō* (2127) and comes from *eu* (2095) which means "good"; and *logéō* (n.f.), to speak, akin to *lógos* (3056), word. It means to speak well of. When the Lord blesses, good things happen. The worlds—all creation in fact—were spoken into existence by the Lord Jesus' words. The apostle Paul wrote, "For by Him were all things created, that are in heaven, and that are in earth" (Col. 1:16).

When Jesus saw the multitude, He saw their spiritual needs and also their physical needs (see Matt. 4:23). He preached and He fed the hungry, and if the sick were present, He healed them too. He met human needs as He came across them.

The doctor uses the available means to help us. Sometimes it is medication, sometimes it is surgery, sometimes it is a modified diet. Jesus did not need to use any means at all. He is sovereign, for He spoke the worlds into existence. Peter calls Him the "Prince [or author] of life" (Acts 3:15), for He can do with a simple word, with *eulogéō,* what no one else can do because of who He is, not because of which words He uses. The words themselves are not magical.

Jesus' healing was done in the context of His preaching. It says in Matthew 9:35, "And Jesus went about all the cities and villages, teaching in their synagogues, and preaching the gospel of the kingdom, and healing every sickness and every disease among the people."

Observe that Jesus' primary role was to preach the gospel. If you recall our previous study of Luke 4, you will remember that Jesus never proclaimed that He came to eliminate sickness. Sickness is ever with us. The people who heard Him that Sabbath day may have wished Him to be a physician (Luke 4:23), but He saw Himself as the predicted Prophet (Luke 4:24).

Now notice Matthew 8:16 which says, "When the even was come, they brought Him many that were possessed with devils: and He cast out the spirits with His word (*lógos*) and healed all that were sick."

If you recall the woman of Canaan in Matthew 15:22–28 who pleaded with the Lord to heal her daughter, you will also recall that she called out for mercy. Mercy cannot be demanded. God can be merciful in healing, and it's perfectly proper to ask for it, but a spirit that demands to be given what one wants is sinful. We must say, "Thy will be done" (Matt. 6:10) and mean it.

We may think that healing is the most merciful thing the Lord could do for us or our loved one. God may restore our health, but then we may find more heartaches which we would have never had to pass through had we not been healed. While we have the freedom to express our human needs to God, we must rest and depend on His sovereign will to do all things well (Mark 7:37) for our ultimate benefit (Rom. 8:28).

Sometimes Jesus Used His Hands (*Cheír*); at Other Times He Took Hold of (*Kratéō*), and Sometimes He Touched (*Háptomai*)

If you followed Jesus around and tried to find a method or plan to His healing that you could try to duplicate, you would become frustrated. The Lord Jesus was not uniform. He could speak, as we have just seen, and the diseases would disappear, but He did not do it that way all the time. If He had, we would have deified the method and shifted our eyes away from the Person of the Lord Jesus Christ. That would be idolatry.

In Matthew 9:18 a synagogue ruler said to Jesus, "My daughter is even now dead: but come and lay Your hand upon her, and she shall live." The word for "hand" is *cheír* (5495). We get our word "chiropractor" from it. Jesus sometimes used touch to heal.

So, even though I am not Jesus, I can give a shoulder rub or a helping hand. God has given us hands to bless others. That is why James wrote, "Someone is sick among you, invite the elders of the church and apply the oil" (James 5:14, a.t.). The word "apply" is *aleíphō* (218), to rub. Your hands are used, but they do not have the same power that Jesus' hands had.

Later on in Matthew 9, Jesus came to the synagogue ruler's house (v. 23) and "took her [the maid] by the hand, and the maid rose" (v. 25). The word "took" is *kratéō* (2902). It means to grasp, lay hold of, or apprehend. It refers to the strong use of a person's hands.

You see, people believed that the touch had power to heal. In Matthew 8:3, Jesus was approached by a leper who wanted to be healed. Matthew records, "And Jesus put forth His hand and touched him." The word for "touch" here is *háptomai* (680). It is not a mere touch; it means to influence the person touched or to be influenced by the person touched. It is the same word Jesus used when Mary Magdalene was told, "Touch Me not; for I am not yet ascended to My Father" (John 20:17).

We have said this earlier but it bears repeating—there is no physical act which a person can do which will help to earn one's salvation. You can make the sign of the cross, take communion, or be baptized, and none of these acts (or any other) will make your relationship right with God. Even Jesus' touch upon the sick was symbolic since we know that He could have merely said the word and the illness would flee.

Some teachers have told people to touch the television or some special cloth they have sent (for a donation) which supposedly had supernatural power to save or heal. This is all wrong. Touch is one of the methods Jesus used, but it is not the only method. Perhaps you should ask yourself if such teachers are willing to use the other methods Jesus used which we are about to look at.

Sometimes He Used His Saliva (*Ptúō*)

Have you ever noticed how much variety Jesus used in His healing methods? It is obvious that Jesus was varying His methods for a reason. Sometimes He spoke, sometimes He took hold of people, sometimes He touched, and now we see that sometimes He spat.

Why don't today's faith healers use spit? If they want to imitate Jesus' methods, why not this one? It is too repulsive for people to accept, that is why. Nobody would come forward to be spit on! Why not sell bottles of "miracle spit"? Would there be a market for it out there?

Mark's gospel records how a deaf and dumb man was healed. He recorded that Jesus "took him aside from the multitude, and put His fingers into his ears, and He spat, and touched his tongue" (Mark 7:33). The word for "touched" is, again, *háptomai,* that is, to be influenced by touch. The Greek for "spit" is *ptúō* (4429).

It is foolish to expect that if we do the same thing that Jesus did, we can have the same results. We forget that the Lord Jesus Christ is sovereign. He decides when and how He wants to heal. Remember Luke 4:27 where Jesus reminded the people that only one leper was healed by Elisha? Was God incapable of healing then? No. He was, is, and always will be sovereign. God chooses who and how many are healed. Again, in John 5 we note that only one man out of many sick was healed. He did not have faith in Jesus until after he was healed (v. 15).

Notice, too, in Mark 7:33, that Jesus purposely took the deaf and dumb man away from the crowd and healed him privately. How unlike this method is from the faith healers today. They promote and advertise greatly. Why did Jesus do it alone and away from the crowd? It was because He did not want His primary program to be interrupted, and that program was to preach the gospel as He said in Luke 4:18.

Jesus was not a publicity or money seeker. He did not take multiple offerings; He healed without cost! He knew the opposition from religious leaders would materialize quickly. Notice that it was Lazarus' resurrection that caused the Pharisees to finally organize to put Jesus to death. John 11:46 says, "But some of them went their ways to the Pharisees, and told them what things Jesus had done." Publicity too early would have been the wrong timing, and Jesus was in control.

Sometimes He Used Mud (*Pēlós*)

This is yet another example of the variety of methods used by the Lord to heal. We have seen Him heal by just speaking, by touching, by spitting, and now we see Him do something even more unusual. He makes clay or mud out of His own spit and dirt. Do we see mud or clay used by healers out there today? Does anyone you know of advise you to spit into some dirt and make clay or mud for healing today?

In John's gospel, the apostle records the following, "He spat on the ground, and made clay of the spittle, and He anointed the eyes of the blind man with the clay" (John 9:6). The word for "clay" is *pēlós* (4081). It's the same word that Paul used in Romans 9:21 where he says, "Has not the potter power over the clay?"

This brings up the issue of whether a Christian should go back to the New Testament in the original language. Some claim that they do not need to understand grammar for the Holy Spirit to teach them. Now while the Holy Spirit is unlimited and can do whatever He wants, He will not teach anyone to read and write when they have an opportunity to go and learn it in school. We have no right to despise the ordinary means at our disposal. We have no right to despise the gift of teachers which the Lord has given to the church (Eph. 4:11).

So when we look at John 9:6–7, we notice that Jesus not only put mud on the blind man's eyes, He also told him to wash in the pool of Siloam. Here we have another element of variety in His methods. There was no healing quality in the mud or in the pool of Siloam. It was in the One who put the mud on him.

It also says He "anointed" him with the mud. The word is *epichríō* (2025) from *epí* (1909), upon; and *chríō* (5548), a sacred anointing. It is the only place other than John 9:11 that this word occurs in the New Testament. This was a sacred anointing by the Son of God.

Sometimes He Healed Progressively (*Pálin*)

In Mark 8 we have a situation which is unique in all the recorded miracles of our Lord. It seems Jesus was intent on forcing His followers to abandon hope of imitating His methods.

It says in Mark 8:22, "And He cometh to Bethsaida." There are three towns that almost form a triangle in the region north of the Sea of Galilee—Capernaum, Chorazin, and Bethsaida. This is where Jesus concentrated most of His ministry. Some people brought a blind man to Jesus and asked if He would touch him. Jesus wanted to throw the emphasis off of the method He used, so He "led him out of the town, and when He had spit on his eyes" (v. 23). He literally spit on his eyes.

What were the results? Have you ever gone from a dark room into the bright sunshine? It takes time to adjust your eyes to the light. This blind man had not fully adjusted to his new sight, because he said, "I see men as trees, walking" (v. 24).

Mark says, "After that He put His hands again upon His eyes, and made him look up: and he was restored, and saw every man clearly" (v. 25). It is that little word "again," which in Greek is *pálin* (3825), which is very interesting. This is the only recorded example of a two-stage effect that the Lord performed. For those of you who take prescription medication, it is often necessary to take it more than once (*pálin*) according to your doctor's orders. The Lord may be sovereignly using it to heal you progressively.

There is a great lesson to be learned here: the Lord heals instantly at times and progressively at other times. The fact that it is progressive does not make it a lesser miracle of God's mercy. Whether a medicine actually works on your situation is sovereignly up to the Lord's will. He is the selective One.

Always He Is Lord (*Kúrios*)

Why do we find such variety in the Lord's healings? Why is there such a constant change in methodology? All the miracles Jesus performed were to prove that He was God. They were signs of His true identity. The various methods He used were designed to shift our focus off of the methods—off of the miracles—and onto the Person who did them.

After Jesus' first miracle in Cana at the wedding feast, the apostle John wrote, "This beginning of miracles did Jesus in Cana of Galilee, and manifested forth His glory; and His disciples believed on Him"

(John 2:11). The word "miracles" is *sēmeía* (4592) or signs. They indicated who this Jesus really was. He was the *Kúrios* (2962); He was the Lord.

When people say, If Jesus did it, I can do it, it is an affront to the Lord. You are not the Lord. He was the God-Man. There are ways for us to use our hands to help, but our hands are not His hands. You see, a doctor can use his hands to remove a cancer, or a woman can clean someone's home, and both can be an act of worship to Christ. We may not be able to heal with our touch, but certainly we can be a blessing with our touch.

Another thing we may learn from the methods of Jesus is that it is no sin, when we are sick, to seek a doctor or take an aspirin. We are free to use the means at our disposal. When Jesus healed, He often used ordinary means, but it was still a healing. When our doctor prescribes an antibiotic, we must keep in mind that the Lord (*Kúrios*) is sovereign. One person takes the medicine and is healed; another takes it and dies. What makes the difference? That is the wrong question! It should be, Who makes the difference? Jesus is always *Kúrios*—He is always Lord.

In John 9:6 it says Jesus "anointed" the blind man's eyes with the mud made with spit. The word "anoint" is *epichríō*. The base word is *chríō*, a sacred word which refers to the relationship that exists between the one who anoints and the one anointed. But observe that the word "anoint" in James 5:14 is not *chríō*, but *aleíphō*, which means to rub. We are to apply the medicine, and the Lord sovereignly decides whether it will work or not. We are not Jesus, but Jesus can, did, and does use means to heal. He is always *Kúrios;* He is always Lord.

15

Prophets, Pentecost, and Miracles

We have been examining carefully the means the Lord Jesus Christ used to heal when He was here on earth and have seen how varied were His methods. After He left us and ascended to the Father, the Holy Spirit came down to indwell the lives of all believers. This was, of course, the event called "Pentecost."

Pentecost was a unique event recorded in Acts 2, and we find that every believer there that day experienced it. It says in verse 4, "And they were all filled with the Holy Ghost, and began to speak with other tongues, as the Spirit gave them utterance." There was what sounded like a rushing wind (v. 2), and what appeared to be fire came upon each one of them (v. 3). But the interesting thing is that no healing miracles were recorded by Luke. Also note that none of the believers who were gathered together there in Jerusalem failed to experience the baptism of the Holy Spirit.

There are some who teach today that if a person is really baptized with the Holy Spirit he will inevitably be able to perform miracles of healing. There is, as we have seen earlier, a kind of arrogance that sometimes accompanies this idea. It is as if we ourselves can control events and make the Lord a "cosmic bellhop" or "spiritual genie" ready to do what we want at our command. This view easily promotes a demanding spirit.

Joel's Prophecy of "the Last Days" (Acts 2:17)

After the miraculous event of tongues, the people "were all amazed, and were in doubt, saying one to another, what means this? Others mocking said, These men are full of new wine" (Acts 2:12–13). In response, the apostle Peter was quick to point out two things: It was too early in the day to be drunk, and what they were witnessing was the fulfillment of Old Testament prophecy, specifically in the book of Joel.

It is important to clarify the prophet Joel's phrase, "the last days." The phrase does not mean the closing days. There are two different words that need to be understood. One is *éschatos* (2078) from which we get the word "eschatology." This is the study of the dispensation of grace which extends from the incarnation of Christ to the very end, including the millennium and the judgment of God. So far, it has been two-thousand years long.

The other word is *hústeros* (5306) from which we get the words "hysterical" and "hysterectomy" and means "the cutting off of the last part." A form of the word is translated "afterward" (5307) in Hebrews

12:11 which says, "Now no chastening for the present seems to be joyous, but grievous: nevertheless afterward it yields the peaceable fruit of righteousness unto them which are exercised thereby."

The word used in Acts 2:17 is not *hústeros* but *éschatos.* Joel is not referring to the very end, the termination day, but to the days beginning with the incarnation of Christ and continuing until Christ comes back again, which is a long period of time.

The word "day" is *hēméra* (2250) and does not necessarily mean a twenty-four hour period, but merely a designated period of time. For example Paul wrote, "Behold, now is the accepted time; behold, now is the day of salvation" (2 Cor. 6:2). We urge people now in this day of grace to repent and believe.

Also, we should not be confused here about the Holy Spirit. Peter quotes Joel as saying, "I will pour out of my Spirit." We should be careful lest we get the idea that the Spirit was not present before Pentecost. The Holy Spirit is co-equal with the Father and the Son from all eternity. Remember, David cried out, "Take not Thy Holy Spirit from me" (Ps. 51:11), but the Spirit is imparted in different ways at different times of history. God accomplishes different things and His methods change, even though He does not change in His essential nature. Remember what Malachi recorded: "I am the Lord, I change not" (3:6).

One of the problems people have today is a shortcoming in biblical understanding. They confuse God's timing in the area of healing. What God does today, He did not have to do before, nor is He required to do tomorrow. We recognize this in dealing with our children. At different points in their lives we treat them differently. We closely control their behavior when they are very young, but with increased age we expect more maturity and wise decisions on their part.

God is working for the salvation of the human race. He is working to re-establish the relationship between humanity and Himself. Thus at Pentecost we see the incredible expansion of the Holy Spirit's influence in the world to save men. This is the baptism in the Spirit. This was the abundance of the Spirit which came on the believers in Jerusalem. This is the formation of the body of Christ.

It is significant that this happened to all the believers present, for Luke said, "They were *all* filled with the Holy Ghost" (Acts 2:4). Paul confirmed this when he wrote, "For by one Spirit are we *all* baptized into one body . . . and have been *all* made to drink into one Spirit" (1 Cor. 12:13).

The Dawn: "I Will Pour Out in Those Days of My Spirit" (Acts 2:18)

We have already noted that at Pentecost there were no recorded healings, but what actually did happen? One thing recorded is that the believers were speaking in languages which they had not learned.

In our day, in our theological world, some are equating the languages spoken at Pentecost with the discordant, disruptive gibberish that created confusion in Corinth. They cannot, however, be equated.

There are some rather obvious differences. For example, at Pentecost there was no need for any translator because the people said, "We hear every man in our own tongue" (Acts 2:8). In Corinth there was a definite need for a translator since Paul's instruction was to "Let one interpret" (1 Cor. 14:13, 27).

Another difference is that whenever an unlearned language was spoken, it was always in the presence of an apostle. You see, this highlights the unique status of the apostolic office. Paul spoke of this when he said, "Truly the signs of an apostle were wrought among you in all patience, in signs, and wonders, and mighty deeds" (2 Cor. 12:12). Notice that these are signs or marks of an apostle, not the average Christian. Just because Paul or Peter could do something does not mean that we can do the same. We cannot write inspired Scripture, can we? No, and we are not apostles able to do miracles.

Another difference was that the languages at Pentecost were authentic human languages. The word "tongue" in Acts 2:8 is *diálektos* (1258) which is translated "language" in "Every man heard them speak in his own language" (Acts 2:6). These are real ethnic languages listed by regions in verses 9 to 11. Over twelve languages were clearly recognized that day.

But the word for "tongues" is *glṓssais* (1100) in verse 11 which says, "We do hear them speak in our own tongues." It is synonymous with *diálektos* from which comes "dialect" in English. When the word *glṓssa,* however, is used in the singular by the apostle Paul in his discussion in 1 Corinthians 12 and 14, he is referring to an unknown, ecstatic gibberish practiced in the confusion at Corinth.

Joel's prophecy continued with "and your sons and your daughters shall prophesy." This does not say anything about tongues, does it? Tongues as untaught human languages were only given for that time. God wanted them to understand the gospel, so He performed a miracle which not only did that but verified the apostles as God's recognized and authenticated spokesmen. He did miracles for the Israelites when they wandered in the desert. He made manna, which He also caused to cease when they entered the promised land. He gave them "wear-ever shoes." He gave them water out of a rock. The Lord performed miracles for them, but He does not do the same miracles for everybody every time using the same methods.

It is also very important to note that the word "prophesy" in verses 17 and 18 means "to forth tell" as well as "foretell." In Joel's prophecy, though, there is no mention of tongues, because tongues merely assisted in an auxiliary way to broadcast the gospel message.

The same can be said about healing. We have seen earlier that the central focus of Jesus' ministry was His message of the gospel. He came to preach the gospel, not primarily to heal. Healing was an added work to focus, not on the sign, but on the "Doer" of the sign.

Thus at Pentecost we have the dawn of that long period between Christ's incarnation and His Second Coming. That dawn is the baptism of the Spirit. This fulfilled the promise given by Jesus to the disciples in John 16:8–11: "And when He is come He will reprove the world of sin, and of righteousness, and of judgment: Of sin, because they believe not on Me; of righteousness, because I go to My Father, and you see Me no more; of judgment, because the prince of this world is judged." Salvation is the primary purpose—the ultimate healing. Physical healing is incidental to the saving work of the gospel. God gave these special ethnic languages at Pentecost in an incidental way to encourage the spread of the gospel.

What we must remember is that a prophecy does not necessarily point to one particular event or one particular time. One prophecy may refer to a length of time or a number of events that will take place. Peter applied Joel 2:28–32 to three different times during the period we refer to as the dispensation of grace. Some are wrongly taking this prophecy of Joel and putting it all into the events of Pentecost when only a part of it applied then.

We have seen how this miraculous language was given at Pentecost, but there is yet another issue which we must learn from this event—languages at Pentecost were not only a blessing, but they were also a curse.

Remember the Tower of Babel in Genesis 11? When men arrogantly and unitedly sought to "make us a name" (v. 4), God sent a curse on the people in the form of divisive languages. Diverse tongues are not a real blessing. Pentecost was a reminder to the people of Israel of God's judgment for rejecting the Messiah.

The Day: "And I Will Show Wonders . . . and Signs " (Acts 2:19)

Here we begin the portion of Joel's prophecy which has not yet taken place. Joel predicted "wonders" (*térata* [5059]), that is, something out of the ordinary. There is a division of science called teratology which studies abnormalities in nature.

Peter is telling us that abnormal things will happen in the heavens involving the stars and planets, and so forth There will someday be a disturbance in the precision of the heavens causing celestial abnormalities.

In Acts 2:20 Peter tells us, "The sun shall be turned into darkness, and the moon into blood." This will not be a normal solar or lunar eclipse. The sun will be turned off! That's abnormal! It has never happened except when Jesus Christ was hanging on the cross. The word for "darkness" is *skótos* (4655) which means the essence of darkness.

But Joel (and Peter) continue with "signs in the earth beneath" (v. 19). The word for "signs" is *sēmeía* (4592). *Sēmeíon* is "a miracle with an ethical end and purpose. Signs are valuable not so much for what they are as for what they indicate of the grace and power of the doer" (see word 4592 in the author's *Hebrew-Greek Key Study Bible,* Lexical Aids to the New Testament). Why "signs"? Because they point to what the Lord is accomplishing on the earth to redeem it in its completeness. It is what Paul means when he says, "For He must reign, till He has put all enemies under His feet" (1 Cor. 15:25).

There are people who take the prophecy of Joel and refer it to the one event of Pentecost exclusively. They force the wonders and signs into this time frame saying it is not for the future, claiming the wonders and signs are their supposed healings. The problem is that the past cannot be brought into the present, nor can the future be forced into the present.

Thus the phrase, "the day of the Lord" in verse 20, technically means the day that God is going to bring punishment upon the earth. It is the tribulation period of seven years prophesied by the prophet Daniel, and the events described here in Acts 2:19–20 that have not occurred yet.

This desire to place wonders and signs into the present is leading some to teach that the gospel must be accompanied by such events, or people will not be truly saved. They say their signs and wonders are the recovery of the Spirit's work at Pentecost. Some even name their ministries, "Signs and Wonders."

The radical difference between the wonders and signs Joel predicted and the miracles of the apostles is clear when closely examined. The natures of the types of miraculous events are different. Their location is different, too. One major difference is that Joel's events are universal in nature. The apostolic miracles and even the miracles of our Lord Jesus were relatively local. No one in the Americas saw them. No one in China saw them.

Methods change. The way God works can change. What we have in Acts 2:18–20 are the wonders and signs that will take place when the Lord comes back. In reality, the signs and wonders performed by Jesus and the apostles did not complete the task of persuading people to repent.

This is especially true of Israel. Paul's great desire was for his nation—the people of Israel—to be saved. "Brethren, my heart's desire and prayer to God for Israel is that they might be saved" (Rom. 10:1). He later wrote, "and so all Israel will be saved" (Rom. 11:26).

The Dusk: "Before That Great and Notable Day of the Lord Comes" (Acts 2:20)

These tremendous wonders and signs which Joel and Peter wrote about will be "immediately after the tribulation of those days" as Jesus taught in the Olivet Discourse (Matt. 24:29). This is the tribulation time before which the Lord Jesus will take those who are believers unto Himself. That is why Paul could write, "Wherefore comfort one another with these words" (1 Thess. 4:18). That is called the Day of Christ. All believers—the dead who will be raised and the living—will be transformed and will meet the Lord in the air. The Lord will show His wrath on unregenerate humanity, but never on His people (1 Thess. 5:9). That wrath has been already endured by Christ on the cross.

After this tribulation, "The sun will be darkened, and the moon shall not give her light, and the stars shall fall from heaven, and the powers of the heaven shall be shaken" (Matt. 24:29). Have these things happened yet? No. But they will because the Lord Jesus Christ said, "And then shall appear the sign of the Son of man . . . coming in the clouds of heaven with power and great glory" (Matt. 24:30).

This is the time when the Lord will return, not for His saints but with His saints (Col. 3:4), and so it is called "the great and notable day of the Lord" (Acts 2:20). The word for "notable" is *epiphanḗs* (2016) which comes from *phaínō* (5316), meaning to shine. The word *epiphanḗs* means glorious or illustrious. Every eye will focus upon the greatness of this day. Nobody will be able to escape it.

When Peter quoted Joel 2, he left out verse 32 which reads, "And it shall come to pass, that whosoever shall call on the name of the Lord shall be delivered: for in Mount Zion and in Jerusalem shall be deliverance, as the Lord has said, and in the remnant whom the Lord shall call." This brings to mind what Paul wrote in reference to Israel: "Even so then at this present time also there is a remnant according to the election of grace" (Rom. 11:5). So when Paul says, "all" in "And so all Israel shall be saved" (Rom. 11:26), the "all" refers to all of that remnant, that is, all in that remnant will be saved.

When the universal miracles come of which our Lord speaks in Matthew 24:29 and which are predicted in Joel 2 and Acts 2, every soul that calls upon the name of the Lord will be saved. The preaching of the gospel universally that is prophesied in Matthew 24:14 is for that particular time.

Present or Future Time?

There are those today who either state or imply that those who do not exercise the power of healing do not have the Holy Spirit. They say that if a person has the Holy Spirit, he should be able to do signs and wonders, as they claim they do.

But this betrays a lack of careful observation of the Scriptures which are our only reliable source of truth about spiritual realities. As a result, some very basic facts are being ignored. Prophecy that deals with events of the future are wrongly transplanted into the present. There is a failure to see that healing is not even mentioned either in Joel's prophecy or in the events recorded about Pentecost. There is also an underlying failure to note that God works in different ways with different people at different times. This "signs and wonders" mentality springs from an insubordinate attitude toward our sovereign Lord and makes Him into our celestial "errand boy."

How important it is to carefully observe our Bible for what it truly teaches! May the Holy Spirit of Pentecost open our eyes to the truths that are in His inspired Word. As Peter wrote, "For the prophecy came not in old times by the will of man: but holy men of God spake as they were moved by the Holy Ghost"

(2 Pet. 1:21). We dare not study the Word with less dependence on the Holy Spirit than the men who were inspired to write it by that same Holy Spirit.

16

Why Were Healings Important in Christ's Ministry?

We know that the Lord Jesus Christ did miracles out of His love for people. When He saw the hungry, the sick, and the demon-possessed, Scripture tells us that He felt compassion for them and reached out to them. But there was also another reason for those miracles which carried over as the underlying reason for the miracles the apostles performed. Here we shall begin to look at healing in the apostolic age.

The Lord of the Apostles: "All That Jesus Began to Do" (Acts 1:1)

Dr. Luke is, of course, the author of both the Gospel of Luke and the book of Acts. It is interesting to note that Luke began his record of apostolic activity with, "The former treatise have I made, O Theophilus, of all that Jesus began both to do and to teach." So Luke's record is really a continuation of what Jesus had started, his point being that Jesus was working through His chosen representatives to continue His work in the world.

At Pentecost, Peter also made a very important link to the ministry of the Lord Jesus. He says in Acts 2:22, "You men of Israel, hear these words; Jesus of Nazareth, a man approved of God among you by miracles and wonders and signs." Peter points to the ministry of the Lord Jesus and tells people that there was an underlying reason for those miraculous events. They were designed to give credibility to the words and person of the Lord Jesus Christ.

The Lord Himself stressed His works to John the Baptist when he had expressed some doubts about the identity of Jesus: "Go and show John again those things which you do hear and see: The blind receive their sight, and the lame walk, the lepers are cleansed, and the deaf hear, the dead are raised up, and the poor have the gospel preached to them" (Matt. 11:4–5).

So Peter was thus reaffirming the basic reason for the Lord's miracles. As we examined Peter's quote from the prophet Joel, we saw Peter ended it with, "Whosoever shall call on the name of the Lord shall be saved" (Acts 2:21). This is true at any time in human history. When Abraham called on the Lord, he was saved, as Jesus indicated in John 8:56, "Your father Abraham rejoiced to see My day: and he saw it, and was glad."

The Proof of the Apostles: "Many Signs and Wonders" (Acts 2:43)

We have already noted that at Pentecost there was the miracle of speaking in ethnic languages without any normal training. We saw how some reacted to that miracle, and how Peter quoted Joel and spread out future history for us. We also noted that no miracles of healing were recorded that day.

In Acts 2:43 are recorded the words, "And fear came upon every soul: and many wonders and signs were done by the apostles." What was the purpose of these apostolic signs? To point to the special commission which they exclusively received from the Lord's hand. Notice that it does not say that these signs and wonders were done by the average Christian.

There were over one hundred and twenty people present on the day of Pentecost. The mother of Jesus was there. His brothers and His family were also there, as Acts 1:14 records: "These all continued with one accord in prayer and supplication, with the women, and Mary the mother of Jesus, and with His brethren."

However, we do not find Mary doing miracles, or Jesus' brothers, or anyone else except the apostles. The reason for this was that the apostles were a very special and specific group of men commissioned directly by the Lord. Now, if the power of healing was to be exercised as a general ability by all believers, you would think we would find some record of a divine healing performed by either Mary or the Lord's brothers.

Peter pointed out in Acts 1:22 that the qualifications for being an apostle include being "ordained to be a witness with us of His resurrection." An apostle had to have seen Jesus raised from the dead and had to be chosen directly by the Lord as one of His followers (v. 21).

The apostle Paul noted in his own ministry that he had the validating signs of an apostle. He said, "Truly the signs of an apostle were wrought among you in all patience, in signs, and wonders, and mighty deeds" (2 Cor. 12:12). He repeated his apostolic credentials in Romans 15:18–19 where he wrote, "I will not dare to speak of any of those things which Christ has not wrought by me . . . through mighty signs and wonders, by the power of the Spirit of God."

So, miracles and signs were the evidence of apostleship and not a sign or evidence for just any Christian, whether or not they were present on the day of Pentecost.

The Procedure of the Apostles: "Peter and John Went Up" (Acts 3:1)

The very first miracle recorded after the day of Pentecost occurred in the temple and is recorded in Acts 3:1–9. What lessons can we learn from how Peter and John worked? Remember that we must observe carefully prior to drawing conclusions.

As we read Acts 3, we observe that Peter and John went up to the temple at the hour of prayer. Did they go there in order to perform healings? It says in Acts 3:1, "Now Peter and John went up together into the temple at the hour of prayer, being the ninth hour." That's about 3:00 p.m. They, of course, did not go into the temple itself, but the temple courtyard. Notice that they went there to pray, but a lame man lay there begging.

Luke notes: "And Peter, fastening his eyes upon him with John, said, Look on us." Just as Jesus could not ignore the suffering of people around Him, so His apostles could not ignore the needs of people either.

Peter and John did not go out of their way to hold a "healing service" and invite the lame man to come, but they did not go away without helping him either. The principle we must learn from this is that we should do whatever we are able to do, and to refuse to help is a sin. The apostle John would later write, "But whoso has this world's good, and sees his brother have need, and shuts up his bowels of compassion from him, how dwells the love of God in him?" (1 John 3:17).

There is yet another principle to consider here. We had better have a proper judgment about who we really are. If we think that because the apostles could heal, then we should be able to do so, too, we will only frustrate or deceive ourselves. Paul told us this directly in Romans 12:3 where he wrote: "For I say, through the grace given unto me, to every man that is among you, not to think of himself more highly than he ought to think; but to think soberly, according as God has dealt to every man the measure of faith." Then Paul lists various spiritual gifts, and "apostleship" is not on the list!

Yet there are those who have commissioned themselves as "apostles" and have even added that title to their names. They imagine themselves as having the same gifts and the same assignment as the original apostles, but there is nothing in Scripture to back up their claims. We have already noted that in Acts 2:43 it tells us that the apostles, not the Christians in general, performed "wonders and signs." This is corroborated in Acts 4:33 which says, "And with great power gave the apostles witness of the resurrection of the Lord Jesus: and great grace was upon them all."

Yet again, another principle can be gleaned from this event: Peter was not self-centered in his thinking. He said, "You men of Israel, why marvel you at this? Or why look you so earnestly on us, as though by our own power or holiness we had made this man to walk?" (Acts 3:12). "Healers" who focus on themselves are not exhibiting apostolic humility.

The Focus of the Apostles: "Whom God Has Raised from the Dead" (Acts 3:15)

This verse leads naturally into noticing what the apostles considered to be the most important Person and event in history. Here the apostle Peter performs a great miracle and, of course, the crowds become excited. Verse 11 records that "all the people ran together unto them in the porch that is called Solomon's, greatly wondering."

We see that Peter gave all the credit to the Lord Jesus and moved the people's thinking away from this miracle to the far greater and more significant miracle of the resurrection of the Lord. He used this miracle to point to the empty tomb by saying, "The God of our fathers has glorified His Son Jesus . . . whom God has raised from the dead" (vv. 13, 15). The resurrection is the greatest proof of the Messiahship of Jesus.

Peter then focuses the crowd's attention on their own personal responsibility. Referring to Jesus, he said, "And His name through faith in His name has made this man strong " (v. 16), but these people had "killed the Prince of life, whom God had raised from the dead; whereof we are witnesses" (v. 15). Peter's purpose was to lead these people to repentance. His intent was to lift up Jesus Christ, not Simon Peter, and so he directs their attention to the resurrection instead of this miracle done by him.

Paul did the same thing in his Mars Hill sermon in Athens. He said: "Because He has appointed a day, in the which He will judge the world in righteousness by that Man whom He has ordained; whereof He has given assurance unto all men, in that He has raised Him from the dead" (Acts 17:31).

You will notice that the apostle Paul, too, had to shift adulation away from himself to the Lord Jesus when he was in Lystra. Paul had healed a lame man (Acts 14:8–10), and the crowd's reaction was an attempt to worship him and Barnabas. The people shouted, "The gods are come down to us in the likeness of men" (v. 11), and they brought sacrifices to offer to Paul and Barnabas (v. 13). Paul and Barnabas tore their clothes and ran among them, begging them not to do it. Luke the physician points out in Acts 4:22 that "The man was above forty years old, on whom this miracle of healing was shown."

When Paul refers to the "gifts of healings" in 1 Corinthians 12:9, he uses the Greek word *íama* (2386). It refers to the result or consequence of something. The word for "gift" is *chárisma* (5486), so in that sense, we are all "charismatics" because as a result of the Holy Spirit's baptism, we all have a gift to be used in His service. We all have a *chárisma.*

But in Acts 4:22, the word is not *íama,* but *íasis* (2392). *Íasis* is the ability to perform a healing. Paul says in 1 Corinthians 12:9 that some people are given gifts to make people well, whereas in Acts 4:22, Luke records that Peter had the actual power or ability to heal people.

It was the apostles' close association with Jesus that the Jewish leaders noted. Luke records this in Acts 4:13–14: "They took knowledge of them that they had been with Jesus. And beholding the man which was healed standing with them, they could say nothing against it."

In Luke 13, Jesus is warned that Herod wants to kill Him (v. 31). Was Jesus worried? No. His response was, "Go you, and tell that fox, Behold, I cast out devils, and I do cures" (v. 32). The word "cures" is *íasis* in the plural. Jesus is declaring His ability and power to heal.

Then Jesus continued, "Today and tomorrow, and the third day I shall be perfected" (v. 32). The Lord would certainly reach His goal which was His resurrection. This was the ultimate sign of His deity. Just as Jesus' miracles pointed to His real identity, so the apostles' miracles pointed to the real identity of Jesus of Nazareth, not to themselves.

The Teaching of the Apostles: "Times of Refreshing . . . Times of Restitution" (Acts 3:19, 21)

In order to understand what the apostles taught, we must carefully note the exact words which they used. For this reason, we refer back to the Greek New Testament and pay heed to the various original words, verbal tenses, and the syntax to give us the needed light.

In Acts 3:19, 21 there are two phrases that Peter employed: "times of refreshing" and "times of restitution." There is no translation available that properly distinguishes the two different Greek words underlying the English word "times" in these two phrases.

The first "time" is *kairós* (2540), and it refers to seasons or opportunities to accomplish a certain purpose. The present age is our *kairós,* our season or opportunity to have our sins forgiven and removed. *Kairós* is closely tied to the word "refreshing" which is *anápsuxis* (403). This word combines *aná* (303), which means "again"; and *psúchos* (5592), which means "cold." So the idea is that of refreshing the person. The only place a person can find spiritual coolness and refreshing is in Jesus Christ. So, now is the *kairós* to find *anápsuxin* in Jesus. When you are sick or facing incredible problems, that may be the event which the Lord has allowed to drive you to Him.

But Peter also said, "And He shall send Jesus Christ" (v. 20). "Shall send" is the aorist subjunctive form of the verb *apostéllō* (649). At a specific time Jesus will come and change us from our present corruptible bodies into permanent, incorruptible bodies. Until then, all our healings that are physical are also temporary. Someday, though, we will have permanent healing.

For this reason, Peter continued, "whom the heaven must receive until the times of restitution" (v. 21). This "time" is not *kairós* but *chrónos* (5550). We get our word "chronology" from it. *Chrónos* is a specific time, not a season. At God's chosen specific time, His *chrónos,* He will reconstitute what has fallen away. This is the eager hope of the Christian which Paul calls "the redemption of our body" (Rom. 8:23).

The Possibilities for Non–Apostles: "Greater Works" (John 14:12)

We made an important point earlier in our study that the apostles were a unique group of men who were especially chosen and commissioned directly by the Lord Jesus. Of course, one implication of this is that no more apostles could exist after the first century. This view is corroborated by the teaching of the apostle Paul in Ephesians 2:20 which says, ". . . and are built upon the foundation of the apostles and prophets." It seems strange to imagine any building that has foundation blocks on the twentieth floor. And it is also strange to imagine new apostles in the present century.

There is a verse, however, that has caused considerable controversy in the Christian world. It is Jesus' words in John 14:12 which say, "Verily, verily, I say unto you, he that believes on Me, the works that I do shall he do also; and greater works than these shall he do; because I go unto My Father."

Does this mean that today's Christian can perform greater miracles than even Jesus did? Let us first notice that Jesus does not say "miracles"; He says "works." The Greek word is *érgon* (2041) which means work, performance, the result of employment (see word 2041 in *Hebrew-Greek Key Study Bible,* Lexical Aids to the New Testament).

What were the "works" of Christ? They included feeding multitudes, the healings, and all His miracles—but they also included the preaching of the gospel of forgiveness. It is interesting that no one in the present century is claiming that he can feed thousands of people with a few loaves of bread!

If a person is able to perform healings, as some now claim, why isn't that same person able to raise the dead? Why are his miracles restricted to just healing? Remember, Jesus did not perform miracles merely to meet a person's need, but also to prove who He was. He was the only one on earth who was not restricted in His miracle-working power, but He gives no mere man the same unrestricted ability.

We must note that even the apostles did not have unrestricted power to do whatever they wanted to do. That is why Peter said, "Why look you so earnestly on us, as though by our own power or holiness we had made this man to walk?" (Acts 3:12). Peter was clear in his words that he did not have either the power or the holiness to effect this miracle. He clearly saw himself as a mere conduit of Jesus' power and holiness. Peter knew that only Jesus could say, "All power is given unto Me in heaven and in earth" (Matt. 28:18). No true apostle would ever claim what Jesus claimed.

The apostles did not have the authority to perform miracles at will and they did not perform as many miracles as Jesus did. Peter walked on water, but he never asked anyone else to do the same. The reason is clear—even an apostle commissioned directly by the Lord is not omnipotent. The prophet Isaiah put it this way, "I am the Lord: that is My name: and My glory I will not give to another " (Is. 42:8). The Lord does not share that power.

So when Jesus said, "greater works," He was referring to works which would be an expansion of His own work. For example, AMG International can provide a ton of rice for about $350. That can feed about five thousand children one meal apiece. So a believer can, instead of using his money selfishly, give it to the Lord's work so that many children can be fed. There are many people who could give $700 to feed over ten thousand hungry people.

We can see this principle at work in the apostle Peter's own experience. After Jesus' ministry, which covered about three-and-a-half years, there were only a few followers who gathered at Pentecost. Yet, over three thousand people came to the Lord as a result of one sermon preached on Pentecost (Acts 2:41)!

Today we have greater opportunities and greater methods to do the work of the Lord than ever before. There has been a tremendous expansion of the work of the Lord Jesus in the world. Whereas Jesus' ministry was restricted to Palestine, He expressly promised "greater works" because He was sending them out saying, "Go ye therefore, and teach all nations" (Matt. 28:19) in "the uttermost parts of the earth" (Acts 1:8). Jesus wants us to grasp the fact that He is not just a Jewish Savior; He is the Savior of the whole world.

17

A Look at Today's Healing Ministries

We will now carefully examine how the apostles functioned in the book of Acts and then compare their methods, goals, and attitudes to today's faith-healing ministries. We must always be submissive to the Word of God in our actions and thoughts. It is not enough to claim to be biblical; we must, in actual practice, submit to the Holy Spirit's inspired record and instructions.

Available for Witness

As we have seen earlier, the miraculous healings of the apostolic company were really incidental to their main emphasis of preaching the gospel to the people. The focus and direction of the apostles was not physical healing, but spiritual healing or salvation. They certainly did not use healings as a means to control people, to generate bigger crowds, or to bring in more money.

We noted earlier that the apostles were the ones who performed these healings because Luke notes in Acts 2:43, "And fear came upon every soul: and many wonders and signs were done *by the apostles."* But notice how these early Christians responded. Verses 44 and 45 tell us that "all that believed were together, and had all things common; and sold their possessions and goods, and parted them to all men, as every man had need." They voluntarily shared. These miracles of God's grace imparted grace to the hearts of these Christians to increase their generosity.

The "gift of the Holy Ghost" (Acts 2:38) made these Christians "givers," too. When we realize that we have been given our salvation as an unmerited gift from God, we share with others. That is why Jesus said, "Freely you have received, freely give" (Matt. 10:8). Surely, we should not charge others for what we ourselves freely received, should we?

Then, in Acts 3, Peter and John go into the temple area without any money. "Silver and gold have I none," they said to a lame man there (Acts 3:6), but they gave a gift to this man which was far greater, for they enabled him to walk and leap for joy (v. 8)!

There is a lesson here for us today. Christians know that there is no such thing as luck or chance. Consequently, then, they realize that the people they come across in the normal course of a day are placed there because of divine providence. When a needy person comes across our path, that is the one we are supposed to help. If they do not know the Lord Jesus Christ, our first priority is to witness to them of their need for spiritual healing, but if they have a physical need, then it is our responsibility to try to do something about it.

We learn such a lesson from the parable of the Good Samaritan recorded in Luke 10:25–37. Should we be satisfied to only pray for a man who is half-dead on the roadway? A believer in Jesus Christ is always enabled to do something more. If nothing else, a word of encouragement and comfort can be given. The Good Samaritan did what he could do, and, as we have earlier noted, if he could have taken him to an emergency room he would have, but he did the next best thing.

Peter used the temple healing as an opportunity to give the whole history of Christ's coming into this world, suffering, dying, and resurrecting, and he turned the lame man's healing around to the declaration of the ultimate miracle of the resurrection of Christ. So Peter was open to the providential leadership of the Lord.

But just because a person is walking by faith and is open to God's sovereign leadership in his life does not mean that everything will automatically go well for him. The next thing that happened to Peter and John was that they were arrested and thrown into prison (Acts 4:1–3)! The local leadership was upset because of Peter's message.

Here we see a tremendous change in Peter from that shaking, quaking "fellow" (Luke 22:54–62) who denied the Lord, to a bold preacher right inside the temple courts. If he had wanted to avoid controversy and prison, he could have done so very easily. All he needed to do was to concentrate on a healing ministry, for that would not offend as the gospel does. But no, Peter knew that preaching and not healing was the main purpose of his work. The apostle Paul said the same thing when he wrote, "For the preaching of the cross is to them that perish foolishness; but unto us which are saved it is the power of God . . . we preach Christ crucified, unto the Jews a stumbling block" (1 Cor. 1:18, 23).

All Peter needed to do to avoid trouble was go with the crowd. The crowd is not interested in the gospel, but they certainly are interested in healing! They can feel their aching backs and want to get rid of the pain, but they are offended to hear that their hearts are sick unto death and all their excuses are unacceptable before God. The gospel is offensive.

It is amazing how few times it is recorded that Simon Peter performed healing miracles. It was just not his focus of ministry, and we must seriously question the validity of a ministry that has its primary focus on something which the apostles considered secondary.

Peter and all the apostles knew that physical healing is, by nature, temporary, a reprieve from the inevitable onslaught of death. Peter's emphasis on the gospel is correct, because the gospel is for eternity.

Another incident of healing is recorded in Acts 9:32–35. Luke records, "And as it came to pass, as Peter passed throughout all quarters, he came down also to the saints which dwell at Lydda. And there he found a certain man named Aeneas, which had kept his bed eight years, and was sick of the palsy." Again we see that Peter did not come down to Lydda expressly to heal someone. But when he did heal someone, what was the result? "And all that dwelt at Lydda and Sharon saw him, and turned to the Lord" (v. 35). They did not turn to Peter.

Trusting God's Ways

We have seen how Peter was used by God to preach the gospel and to heal. As we go through the book of Acts, an important figure named Steven is introduced to us. He is first introduced as one of the original seven selected by the apostles to solve the problem of Greek-speaking widows who were being neglected in their need (Acts 6:1–5).

The qualifications for this task are spelled out in verse 3. They were to be "seven men of honest report, full of the Holy Ghost and wisdom." Stephen was one of these original men and he, in addition to the assigned task of service, was directly commissioned by the apostles, and in verse 8 we read, "And Stephen, full of faith and power, did great wonders and miracles among the people." Earlier, we noted that the apostles did signs and wonders, but here we also see that someone who was directly commissioned by an apostle also performed miracles and signs.

What happened to this godly man? Did he become a world-famous healer? No, he became the first martyr (Acts 7:54–60). What a wasted life, we may think. But what was the greatest good that God could do for Stephen? You see, we focus on the loss which we think occurred as a result of his death, and yet the Lord obviously thought differently.

It is because of Stephen that we are introduced to a young man named Saul (Acts 8:1). Saul had listened to Stephen's sermon recorded in Acts 7:2–53. Luke records the reaction of his listeners that, "When they heard these things, they were cut to the heart, and they gnashed on him with their teeth" (v. 54).

This is not the same reaction as the crowd at Pentecost. Luke, at that point, said, "They were pricked in their heart" (Acts 2:37). This was certainly a different reaction to the gospel.

We cannot always see with the human eye what God is doing in the midst of what we consider a tragedy. The crucifixion of Jesus Christ should teach us that, too. Saul was touched by Stephen. He had gone on a rampage against the church, and ringing in Saul's ears was the last prayer of Stephen: "Lord, lay not this sin to their charge" (Acts 7:60).

Usually in the middle of our problems, we pray for deliverance. We echo the prayer Jesus taught His disciples, "Deliver us from evil" (Matt. 6:13). The word "deliver" is *rúomai* (4506), and it means to draw away with force and violence, to drag or pull (*Hebrew-Greek Key Study Bible,* Lexical Aids to the New Testament). Paul was delivered, or *rúomai,* many times, describing it on one occasion as being "delivered out of the mouth of the lion" (2 Tim. 4:17). Sometimes that may mean we are rescued in a way we hope, but Stephen, through his martyrdom, was delivered too!

Can you imagine how great an honor it is to have Jesus Christ stand up to greet you as you enter Paradise as He did with Stephen (v. 56)? With this thought in mind, we can rest assured, knowing that problems are not always a sign of our Lord's chastening nor a lack of faith on our part.

We must also note another situation that Peter came upon recorded in Acts 9. After he healed Aeneas, he came across the funeral of a young woman named Tabitha (or Dorcas; see Acts 9:36–38). Here we have a faithful believer whose life exhibited the fruit of the Spirit and, as everyone else eventually does, she died. There are some today who would say that she must have committed some heinous sin or she would not have been sick, and if she had sufficient faith, would have been healed and would not have died.

Carrying this to the extreme, such people today could point to Jesus on the cross and chide Him for not having enough faith, either. There were those at the foot of the cross shouting to Jesus and saying, "If You are the King of the Jews, save Yourself" (Luke 23:37). It was the repentant thief who realized that suffering and death did not always mean personal sin or lack of faith (which is also sin). He said, "This Man has done nothing amiss" (Luke 23:41).

The same principle applies to Lazarus of Bethany. There is no implication at all noted in the Scripture that Lazarus was deficient in either faith or practice. We know Jesus' attitude toward him because Lazarus' sisters said to Jesus, "Lord, behold, he whom You love is sick" (John 11:3). And yet Lazarus died. In fact, it appears that Jesus intentionally delayed His arrival in Bethany precisely to allow Lazarus to die so that He could raise him up (John 11:1, 6, 11, 14)! Jesus allowed it to display His glory (John 11:40).

We must come to the point where we trust the Lord in what He sovereignly decides to bring into our lives. We do not demand of Him what we think is the solution to our problem, and we have the right to be suspicious of any ministry that subtly encourages a spirit of dissatisfaction or discontent with the designs of our Savior.

In the case of Dorcas, Peter was used to bring her back to life, and "many believed in the Lord" (Acts

9:42). Peter did not go to the local graveyard to resurrect everybody, either. Nor did Peter focus on himself. He negated his role when the lame man was healed in the temple.

That is another thing we must beware of in today's healing ministries. It is a kind of crass commercialism that has arisen. This is sad because the gospel is really where the focus needs to be. So, be aware, for self-promotion by healers is the opposite of the Christ-promotion of the apostles.

Thinking Correctly

We have observed very carefully what Peter did in the area of physical healing. We have repeatedly seen that his emphasis was not on the physical, but predominately on the spiritual. And it is also appropriate that we examine what he taught in his letters.

Peter did not believe that our present bodies, even as believers, are exempt from suffering and sickness. No one denies, especially Peter, that God can heal anybody at anytime He wishes, but Peter believed that there is going to be a day of physical liberation. He calls it our "salvation"—the salvation of our body (1 Pet. 1:5).

Peter wrote in 1 Peter 1:3, "Blessed be the God and Father of our Lord Jesus Christ, which according to His abundant mercy has begotten us again unto a lively hope by the resurrection of Jesus Christ from the dead." Peter very clearly points out that there was an event which his readers had already shared as a common experience. That event is regeneration or the new birth referred to in the phrase "has begotten us again." It is an aorist participle and signifies a one-time action prior to the next words, "unto a lively hope." "Lively hope" in the Greek is a present participle, emphasizing that our hope is something we continuously enjoy as a result of our regeneration.

The moment we are born-again, we have the Spirit of God within us, but our bodies remain exactly the same. Yet what that new birth does give us is a vibrant hope that someday we will be clothed with a new, perfect body that will be incorruptible. That is why Peter could add, "Who are kept by the power of God through faith unto salvation ready to be revealed in the last time" (v. 5).

So, there is a sense in which we *were* saved when we believed, we *are* saved at present, and we *will be* saved in the future. This last aspect, Peter tells us, will occur "in the last time." Whereas we still have the same body, the day will come when the spirit which God has already begun to renew within us will be joined to a renewed body. Until that time we must be patient for we are passing through God's ordained periods of time (*kairós* [2540]).

Peter is quite specific as to when this is going to happen. In 1 Peter 1:7 he says that our current problems ("the trial of your faith") will be worth it all "at the appearing or revelation of Jesus Christ" when we will have our redeemed, saved body.

Until then, Peter tells us to "gird up the loins of your mind" (v. 13). In those days a person's outer clothing was loose and flowing. When it was necessary to run or fight or work, they would tie up their robes so that they would not trip over them. Today there is a great deal of "loose" and "sloppy" thinking which can trip us up and proves how relevant this verse is to our present time.

In Peter's second letter he tells us, "Brethren, give diligence to make your calling and election sure: for if you do these things, you shall never fall: For so an entrance shall be ministered unto you abundantly into the everlasting kingdom of our Lord and Savior Jesus Christ" (2 Pet. 1:10–11). We have already had an entrance into that kingdom as Paul told us in Colossians 1:13: "Who . . . has translated us into the kingdom of His dear son." The kingdom is not only now, but it is also a future hope.

Peter emphasized this new entrance to which we look forward. He was told by the Lord that he would die (John 21:18–19), and so he wrote, "I must put off this my tabernacle" (2 Pet. 1:14). He regarded his physical body as a mere tabernacle or tent in which his spirit dwelt, much like the temporary traveling tent in the wilderness which the Israelites eventually discarded for the temple. We, too, will leave our tents behind when the Lord gives us glorified bodies.

Recognizing Falsehood

In the Sermon on the Mount, the Lord Jesus taught about the broad way and the narrow way. He then warned His disciples about false prophets when He said, "Beware of false prophets, which come to you in sheep's clothing, but inwardly they are ravening wolves" (Matt. 7:15). The apostle Paul, when giving advice to the Ephesian elders said, "Take heed therefore unto yourselves, and to all the flock. . . . For I know this, that after my departing shall grievous wolves enter in among you, not sparing the flock" (Acts 20:28–29). The apostle John similarly warned, "Beloved, believe not every spirit, but try the spirits whether they are of God: because many false prophets are gone out into the world" (1 John 4:1).

Unbelieving Believers

There is a powerful event recorded in Acts 8:4–25. It is the incident of Philip and Simon Magus. This event should forever settle the issue of whether the Holy Spirit is for sale. So many of today's healers have multiple offerings during their meetings. It is almost the unspoken teaching (and sometimes even spoken openly) that the more you give, the more you can expect the healings and miracles of God to work for you. We once listened to one healer on the radio say that if you don't put any money in the envelope that you send to him, don't expect to get anything from the Lord in return, and if you put in a lot, you can expect to get a lot. Can you buy the "gift of the Holy Spirit"?

Philip, like Stephen, one of the original deacons listed in Acts 6:5, went to Samaria where he performed miracles and preached Christ to the Samaritans (Acts 8:5). This shows that Philip was an official, validated appointee of the Twelve Apostles, and that is why Peter and John came to give their blessing.

Now Simon the Magician is introduced in verses 9 and 10 with the words ". . . Simon . . . used sorcery, and bewitched the people of Samaria, giving out that he was some great one: To whom they all gave heed, from the least to the greatest, saying, This man is the great power of God." Here we find a great weakness which many people have today. It is a prime example of "loose" or "sloppy" thinking. These Samaritans thought that anything that is extraordinary must come from God. This is a very subtle trap.

Miracles are no proof that the doer of them is a true prophet of God, and that is why Jesus said, "Many will say to Me in that day, Lord, Lord, have we not prophesied in Your name? And in Your name have cast out devils, and in Your name done many wonderful works? And then will I profess unto them, I never knew you: depart from Me, you that work iniquity" (Matt. 7:22–23).

It is interesting to note that these "believers" really were not true believers because it says in Acts 8:12 that "they believed Philip." They did not believe in Jesus Christ. They had merely changed from believing in Simon to a greater and better miracle worker. It was a superstitious faith, not saving faith, because it did not have Jesus Christ as its true object.

These people demonstrated a "James 2:19 faith." There James wrote, "You believe that there is one God; you do well: the devils also believe, and tremble." These Samaritans had a "devilish faith" (James 3:15). They had no heart commitment to Jesus as Lord, and no one can have Jesus as Savior and not have Him as Lord also.

This very thing had happened to the Lord Jesus. He had gone to the Passover festival in Jerusalem and "many believed in His name, when they saw the miracles which He did" (John 2:23), but the next verse proves that this was not a real, saving faith. John recorded: "But Jesus did not commit Himself unto them, because He knew all men . . . for He knew what was in man" (vv. 24–25). The same Greek word, *pisteúo* (4100), is translated "believed" in verse 23 and "commit" in verse 24. They really did not believe in Jesus and He really did not believe them either, for He knew that they did not possess genuine, saving faith.

The Samaritans had a "devilish faith," and they needed Peter's apostolic discernment. Simon Magus saw that the apostles could lay hands on people and that, as a result, the Holy Spirit was received (Acts 8:14–18). Simon's reaction indicated his lost condition. He said, "Give me also this power, that on whomsoever I lay hands, he may receive the Holy Ghost" (v. 19). Simon did not see the Holy Spirit as a member of the Trinity, but as a power. Peter strongly reprimanded him by saying, "Your heart is not right in the sight of God" (v. 21).

This is a principle which modern faith healers have sadly forgotten—the Holy Spirit is a gift, He is a part of the Triune Godhead. He cannot be bought. He is not merely or primarily a power one can tap into to solve problems. He is the sovereign Lord, the promised Holy Spirit, not the purchased Holy Spirit.

Profits, Not Prophets

Peter's first letter deals with persecution from outside the church, whereas his second letter deals with error within it. Peter warns in 2 Peter 2 against false teachers because not everybody who holds a Bible in his hand is a true spokesman for God, and Peter does not want the church to be deceived.

In verse 2 Peter says, "And many shall follow their pernicious ways." The word is *asélgeia* (766) in the Majority Greek text and it refers to something that a person can never have enough of. It is the constant need to have more and more of anything, whether money, power, or things. It can include the *asélgeia* to have the power to heal and to present oneself as a healer of all people.

Peter goes on to say, "And through covetousness shall they with feigned words make merchandise of you" (v. 3). The word "covetousness" is translated from *pleonexía* (4124) which in turn is from *pléon* (4119), meaning "more," and *échō* (2192), meaning "to have." These false teachers want more and more. They are never satisfied. Peter also used the word *plastós* (4112) from which we get the English "plastic," meaning it can be molded into various forms. *Plastós* is translated "feigned" and means smooth words. These false teachers are "smooth" talkers and twist words. Whereas they can be heard and understood one way, they mean it another way. In order to get more and more, they try to please everybody.

Peter says that they "make merchandise" (*kapēleúō* [2585], merchandising the Word of God; 2 Cor. 2:17) of the unwary. In other words, they are only using the listener's lack of discernment to make money. Their audience is mere merchandise to them. Sadly, the Christian faith is today being merchandised. Instead of *feeding* the flock, these false teachers are *fleecing* the flock. They may escape the eye of the Internal Revenue Service, but the Lord takes notice, and Peter reassures us that their "judgment now of a long time lingers not, and their damnation slumbers not" (v. 3; see also Rom. 16:17–20).

Here at AMG International people are not receiving large salaries. Profits from books such as the one you are reading are put back into the ministry to help fund programs of evangelism and the meeting of physical needs. It is every Christian's obligation to exercise great discernment as to the organizations they choose to support financially.

There are some who are "servants of corruption" (2 Pet. 2:19). They will promise healing, financial success, and all manner of prosperity if you send them some money. Let us pray that the Lord will show us how to wisely support those who are truly the Lord's servants.

18

Paul's Own Illness

We have seen how the Lord Jesus Christ performed healings and how the apostle Peter was empowered by the Holy Spirit to perform many signs and wonders.

However, in the case of the apostle Paul, many people fail to realize that even he had a physical infirmity that he had to endure. Here was a mighty man of God who saw the Holy Spirit use him to heal others, yet he could not heal himself. In fact, Paul had besought the Lord three times to heal him, and it was denied him (2 Cor. 12:8–9). In this chapter we want to examine what Paul thought of his illness, how the Galatians regarded his illness, and the reason why he was not healed.

"Through Infirmity of the Flesh I Preached the Gospel" (Gal. 4:13)

Our attitudes regarding healing and sickness must be formed by the Scriptures themselves. Of course, the Lord Jesus' attitude, as well as Paul's, Peter's, and John's, are our primary reference points.

When our Lord was crucified, there were those who taunted Him, laughingly suggesting that He come down off the cross if He was the Son of God (see Matt. 27:39–44). Did Jesus have the power to save Himself? Of course He did, but that would have not fulfilled His Father's and His own plan that He should atone for sin. Jesus, being then the God-Man in full submission to His heavenly Father, shed His blood on the cross for the remission of our sins. That was His purpose for coming to earth. Peter said, "Him, being delivered by the determinate counsel and foreknowledge of God, you have taken, and by wicked hands have crucified and slain" (Acts 2:23). It was God's will for Jesus Christ to die.

And it was God's will for the apostle Paul to heal only when the Lord ordained it. He did not have the inherent power to heal anybody at any time. It was only when the sovereign Lord permitted it that he had the power to heal.

We find in Acts 13 that after Paul and Barnabas left Cyprus, they sailed to Perga (v. 13). Perga is a seaport and, according to Ramsey, it was an area infested with malaria-infected mosquitoes. As we have mentioned previously, could it be that Paul had contracted malaria and went up to Galatia, which is about three thousand feet above sea level, for health reasons? This, then, would be where Galatians 4:13 fits in: "You know how through infirmity of the flesh I preached the gospel unto you at the first." Be clear about what the apostle Paul means by "infirmity." The word is *asthéneia* (769), and it is in the accusative case. It is linked with the preposition "through" (*diá*

[1223]). When *diá* is used with the accusative it means on account of or because of. So perhaps Paul is reminding the Galatians of something they fully recognized—he had an illness and was there at a higher altitude for health reasons. Paul is reminding them that circumstances forced a change of plans, possibly forcing him from a trip to Ephesus (at the time a seaport city) to the mountains.

The apostle Paul would understand the song, "Brighten the Corner Where You Are," for Paul eventually landed in a Philippian jail cell (Acts 16:23–30). No one wants to be imprisoned, but Paul knew that prison was just another opportunity disguised as a problem. So he sang and prayed out loud (Acts 16:25), and the Lord sent an earthquake. This alarmed one of the guards who asked, "Sirs, what must I do to be saved?" (Acts 16:30). Paul had been beaten up and was wounded, yet he did not slack in his witness for his Lord.

If you are sick now, you are probably full of questions. You may be asking, Did God put me here in this sickbed? The answer is, God allowed it. Although Satan can cause problems for us, the Lord works them out for our eventual good. Satan is not co-equal with God, and God has set limits to his evil work (see Job 1:8–12; 2:3–10).

In Galatians 4:13, Paul reminds them that "You know [*oídate* {1492}] how through infirmity of the flesh." It means that you understand or come to the conclusion. This infirmity of the flesh was definitely a physical illness, yet he preached the gospel. He is saying that he took the opportunity to preach the gospel even though the first time they heard him he was sick.

Paul knew that the Lord had a purpose for his, and that was to make Him known. Today there are those who wrongly teach that God's purposes could never include sickness (or prison!). Many Christians today are being taught that since they have been forgiven, then all other benefits should be theirs now, also. Consequently, we develop wrong priorities. We become far too self-centered. We are like Narcissus of Greek mythology who fell in love with his reflection in a pool of water and leaned over so far that he fell in and drowned. And wasn't it Absolom's long, beautiful hair that led to his death when it became caught in a tree (see 2 Sam. 18:9)! We are not here primarily to enjoy good health, but to witness to the love of God through Jesus Christ.

"You Despised Not, nor Rejected; but Received Me" (Gal. 4:14)

Here is an interesting situation among the Galatians. Paul comes to them, a man who was in poor health and suffering, and the people do not draw a wrong conclusion. They do not think less of Paul because he is sick. In today's church, he might be disregarded, for some would deduce that Paul is obviously out of favor with the Lord, that he was probably being chastised as a result of some personal sin, and consequently they would reject him.

Paul wrote, "And my temptation which was in my flesh you despised not" (v. 14). The word translated "temptation" is *peirasmós* (3986). Its root is *peíra* (3984) which means "experience." It is perfectly acceptable to render it "temptation" as the King James translation has it for *peirasmós* is an experience which is difficult and which presents us with an opportunity to either listen to the Lord or listen to the flesh.

This same word is used three times in 1 Corinthians 10:13 which says: "There has no temptation taken you but such is as common to man: but God is faithful, who will not suffer you to be tempted above that you are able; but will with the temptation also make a way to escape, that you may be able to bear it." This is penned by a man who knows what he is talking about. We all have these puzzling experiences. The Lord, Paul says, will help you bear your temptation and control it.

Now, there are those who say that Paul's problem was not a physical problem. The Greek text says, however, "in my flesh" (*sárx* [4561]). The New American Standard Version translates it "in my bodily condition" and the New International Version as "my illness." It was a physical sickness.

In spite of this obvious illness, Paul writes, "you despised not." The word "despised" is *exouthenḗs* from *exouthenéō* (1848). The same word is used in Luke 18:9 where the Lord says, "And He spoke this parable unto certain which trusted in themselves that they were righteous, and despised others." It means to show contempt, to depreciate.

Then Paul adds, "nor rejected." This word is *ekptúō* (1609) from *ek,* out of (as in our word "exit") and *ptúō* (4429), to spit. It means to spit out, eject. The word is used in Luke 18:32 in predicting the Lord's mistreatment, "For He shall be delivered unto the Gentiles, and shall be mocked, and spitefully treated, and spit upon" [*emptusthḗsetai* {1716}, a synonym of *ekptúō,* both words from the verb *ptúō,* to spit].

There is a clear procedure or process people follow in coming to rejection. The first step is to have improperly or inaccurately examined the Scriptures. Secondly, as a result, to have a less than biblical idea about the subject. Thirdly, to despise or discount the correct idea when it does come, and finally, to "spit out" the messenger of the idea. This the Galatians did not do.

As a matter of fact, the Galatians "received" Paul. The word for "received" is *edéxasthe,* the second person plural of *déchomai* (1209), to receive. It, means to welcome with open arms. Paul used this same word to command the Colossian church in regard to Mark when he said, "If he come unto you, receive him" (Col. 4:10).

"As an Angel of God, Even as Christ Jesus" (Gal. 4:14)

Paul then describes how the Galatians received him. They "received me as an angel." The word "angel" is *ággelos* (32) which can also mean messenger. In other words, My message to you in my sickness meant more to you than if I were in robust health. The Galatians saw Paul as God's messenger and appreciated him. This is what we fail to grasp today. We do not see that when the minister is sick, his love for the Lord impels him to do for others what he would not normally do when he was feeling well. Paul had this same servant spirit. Some think illness is a result of a lack of faith, whereas it often means great faith. Far too often the church rejects her wounded and shoots down her own soldiers, and this is tragic.

Certainly our Lord did not do that. Matthew 12:20 says, "A bruised reed shall He not break, and smoking flax shall He not quench." Reeds and flax wicks were cheap and disposable, yet the Lord regards something even so insignificant as a crushed reed or an almost burnt-out wick. He does not reject His people and neither should we when problems strike. Too often Christians do the work of three well-known men—Eliphaz, Bildad, and Zophar, Job's friends (Job 2:11)—by adding insults to injury on the head of a suffering fellow saint.

Not only did the Galatians treat Paul as a messenger from God but "even as Christ Jesus." What a significant statement that is in the light of the powerful words of Jesus in Matthew 10:40–41, "He that receives you receives Me, and he that receives Me, receives Him that sent Me. He that receives a prophet in the name of a prophet shall receive a prophet's reward; and he that receives a righteous man in the name of a righteous man shall receive a righteous man's reward." You see, to receive Paul's message even in his weakness was the same as receiving Jesus Christ. If they had rejected Paul based on the externals, they would have rejected the gospel.

This gives us serious food for thought. When our pastor preaches the truth of the Word of God which is inspired by the Spirit of Christ (see 1 Pet. 1:10–11), and we receive that messenger and his messages, it is as though we are receiving Christ. That is true even if his message is delivered in weakness.

It is one thing to praise God when everything is going smoothly, but it is altogether different when in prison (Acts 16:25), sick, or suffering financial reverses. The prophet Habbakuk did just that, saying, "Although the fig tree shall not blossom, neither shall fruit be in the vines; the labor of the olive shall fail, and the fields yield no meat; the flock shall be cut off from the fold, and there shall be no herd in the stalls: Yet I will rejoice in the Lord, I will joy in the God of my salvation" (Hab. 3:17–18). Few of us are spiritually mature enough to do this.

Whether we are sick or healthy, in jail or free, well-off or poor, we are still to witness about our Lord wherever He has providentially placed us. That is what Paul did. That is what Jesus did, even from the cross itself, when He said, "Father, forgive them; for they know not what they do" (Luke 23:34).

"The Messenger of Satan to Buffet Me" (2 Cor. 12:7)

There is a verse in 1 John 5:18 that would seem to open up some serious difficulties if we did not examine it carefully, for he wrote, "We know that whosoever is born of God sins not; but he that is begotten of God keeps himself, and that wicked one touches him not." The "wicked one" referred to here is undoubtedly Satan or the devil. Jesus used similar terminology in Matthew 6:13: "Deliver us from [the] evil [one]," and in John 17:15 in our Lord's "High Priestly prayer," He said: "I pray not that Thou should take them out of the world, but that Thou should keep them from the evil [one]."

What does John mean when he says that the devil cannot "touch" the believer? The word "touch" is *háptomai* (680), and it means to touch so as to leave an influence on a person. This is the same word used in Matthew 9:21 where it says, "For she said within herself, If I may but touch His garment, I shall be whole." She wanted to be influenced through that touch.

One idea made clear in 1 John 5:18 is that Satan cannot put us under his control. The classic biblical example that proves this is found in Job. In Job 2:3 we have these words, "And the Lord said unto Satan, Have you considered My servant Job?" Job was the "servant of God" even before he suffered and during it. When it was all over, the Lord said to Eliphaz, "My wrath is kindled against you, and against your two friends: for you have not spoken of Me the thing that is right, as My servant Job has" (Job 42:7). Then, just to make sure they heard it, the Lord repeated "My *servant* Job" twice more in the next verse. Job was still God's servant in spite of all his trouble.

The Bible does not teach "dualism." That is the belief that teaches that good and evil will battle eternally because they are evenly matched. Not at all! That is one of the main points of Job. Satan is shown to be against God and His people, but God limits his evil influence.

In Ephesians 6:12 Paul uses the word *kosmokrátōr* (2888) which is translated "ruler." This is the only place the word occurs in the entire New Testament. It literally means "world-ruler" (*kósmos* [2889], world; *krátōr,* ruler, from *kratéō* [2902], to hold). Peter refers to Satan as a "roaring lion" (1 Pet. 5:8). He roars, but for the Christian, he has no teeth. What he tries to do is weaken our faith and minimize our ministry. What is truly amazing is that Satan actually encourages our ministry by his tactic. Paul said, "I rather glory in my infirmities, that the power of Christ may rest upon me. . . . for when I am weak, then am I strong" (2 Cor. 12:9–10).

And this is where 2 Corinthians 12:7 fits our discussion of the apostle Paul's views. He wrote: "And lest I should be exalted above measure through the abundance of the revelations, there was given to me a thorn in the flesh, the messenger of Satan to buffet me, lest I be exalted above measure."

Paul, in this letter to Corinth, had been dealing with men who were false prophets (see 2 Cor. 11:13–15). They had bragged that they were "super-apostles" and that Paul was obviously out of favor with the Lord. They apparently boasted about their visions which they supposedly had as proof of their vaunted superiority. Paul finally gives an account of his vision in 2 Corinthians 12:1–6. He hesitated to talk about it (vv. 5–6) and even wrote as if speaking of someone else ("I knew a man " [vv. 2–3]) which shows the deep humility of a true servant and a true apostle.

So Paul says that a physical problem "was given to me" (v. 7). Yes, God does give sickness, but always with a higher purpose. That is why Jeremiah could say, "He has bent His bow, and set me as a mark for the arrow. . . . This I recall to my mind, therefore have I hope. It is of the Lord's mercies that we are not consumed, because His compassions fail not" (Lam. 3:12, 21, 22). Jeremiah and Paul both knew that God brings us closer to Himself through suffering.

So although Satan may afflict us, behind his hand is the hand of God allowing him to go so far and no farther. Satan may be the *kosmokrátōr,* the ruler of the world, but the Lord is the *Pantokrátōr* (3841), the Ruler over all. The prefix *pánta* means "all." This one word most appropriately occurs nine times in the book of Revelation. It is translated "Almighty." History is under the control of the Almighty Lord. That is true in world history as well as in our personal history.

The word *Pantokrátōr,* other than in Revelation, occurs only one other time. In 2 Corinthians 6:18, referring to the promise of fellowship to those who walk godly in the world, Paul wrote, "And you shall be My sons and daughters, says the Lord Almighty." Now, a few chapters later in 2 Corinthians 12, Paul says that this *Pantokrátōr* has allowed the *kosmokrátōr* to send a messenger (literally "angel" [*ággelos*] for Satan's demons are fallen angels) to "buffet" him.

The word "buffet" is *kolaphízō* (2852) which comes from *kólaphos* (n.f.), a blow. This latter word means to correct or punish by punching, to hit or strike with the fist. Paul's thorn in the flesh was a disturbance from the outside. Thorns may be small to the eye, but they certainly get our attention.

The verb *kolaphízō* is used in the gospel accounts to record that Jesus was beaten or "buffeted" by the Roman soldiers (Matt. 26:67; Mark 14:65). Was God the Father using the Romans to afflict Jesus? Yes, but what was the result? Our salvation! Did good come out of evil? Yes, praise God it did! The greatest, most heinous, despicable crime of humanity was the killing of the Lord Jesus Christ. Peter said they "killed the Prince of life," but then he added, "whom God has raised from the dead" (Acts 3:15). Hallelujah!

The promises of Romans 8:28 that "all things work together for good" is only for "them that love God." If you have not seen your need of Jesus Christ as your Savior and asked for His forgiveness, then things are working for your destruction, for Paul also wrote, "But after your hardness and impenitent heart, [you] treasure up unto yourself wrath against the day of wrath and revelation of the righteous judgment of God" (Rom. 2:5). If you have not fled to Christ, you need to do so. The pilgrim in Bunyan's *Pilgrim's Progress* fled from the City of Destruction, and so must you.

19

God's Sovereign Dealings with People

Sometimes we need to examine the whole before we attempt to look at the parts. Impressionistic painting is just like that. If you get too close, all you see are little dots of paint. Frankly, it is unattractive and not beautiful at all! But if you step back a few feet, all those little dots are blended together into a picture you could not see when standing so close. The same is true for the book of Acts. We have been examining the overall picture on this subject of healing in order to draw some conclusions.

The Sovereign Disposing of God's Servants

God has absolute power to do anything, but He does not violate His nature. He uses His power selectively, not always uniformly without modification. We find this in the account of Paul's conversion on the road to Damascus, for example. In this case, the event was very dramatic and even blinded Paul. You, too, can probably state the time you came to

Christ, but it is doubtful that you had the same kind of blinding vision as Paul had.

What happened to Paul after his conversion? In Acts 9:20, Luke recorded, "And straightway he preached Christ in the synagogues." This caused quite a reaction from the Jews who "took counsel to kill him" (v. 23), and so the Christians in Damascus "took him by night, and let him down by the wall in a basket" (v. 25). This is a pretty humiliating way to leave town. It is not very honoring is it?

God does not always do what He is able to do. He allowed Stephen to be martyred (Acts 7:59–60), but He worked a miracle to get Peter out of prison (Acts 12:6–10). His release came after James, the brother of John, was killed by Herod (vv. 1–2). From this, we can learn a vital lesson. Never say that since God liberated one person in the past, He will do the same thing today by liberating us from our problems.

Did the Damascus believers lack faith by lowering Paul down a wall in a basket? No! They used their human ingenuity. If the Lord wants to liberate us through some measure of relief, then follow His leading. We are His servants. Whether we live or die, whether we are sick or well, whether we are free or imprisoned, it all lies in His arranging of our lives. He is the One who makes the ultimate decision.

The Sovereign Dispensing of God's Justice

We have seen that God does not treat His children uniformly but will do that which focuses on His glory and our ultimate benefit. The important words are "free," because He is sovereign, and "ultimate," because from our perspective the problem often appears to be unalloyed pain or disaster.

Now it is also necessary to examine how God treats His enemies. Here, also, the actions of the Lord are variable and His patience with their evil runs out. Herod made a speech one day, as Luke records: "Herod, arrayed in royal apparel, sat upon his throne, and made an oration unto them. And the people gave a shout, saying, It is the voice of a god, and not a man. And immediately the angel of the Lord smote him, because he gave not God the glory: and he was eaten by worms, and gave up the ghost" (Acts 12:21–23). Here the Lord acted directly and swiftly, and "the word of God grew and multiplied" (v. 24). That was the underlying purpose. God can use angels or any other method, as He sees fit. Jesus demonstrated this in His various healing methods. Sometimes He just spoke, He also made and used mud, or He just touched the person He was healing.

In the life of the apostle Paul, as we saw in 2 Corinthians 12, God gave him physical affliction to bless the lives of others. That is why Paul could begin his letter by saying, "Who comforts us in all our tribulation, that we may be able to comfort them which are in any trouble, by the comfort wherewith we ourselves are comforted of God" (2 Cor. 1:4). Apparently Paul knew that we could be poor comforters to our fellow believers if we have not gone through troubles of our own and drawn from God's storehouse of grace and mercy.

Not only in his physical illness, but also when he was in Rome, Paul understood that the Lord was sovereign. He did not assume that because Peter had been released, he would be also. He wrote, "For I am now ready to be offered, and the time of my departure is at hand" (2 Tim. 4:6). We all need to recall from time to time that Joseph was imprisoned for years, James had been killed, and John the Baptist was beheaded for his biblical stand on the issue of immorality. God does not always take away our problems or eliminate our enemies when we want it.

Those today who wrongly teach that if God did something in the past He will do it now are in some pretty illustrious company. The brothers James and John made this mistake. On a trip through Samaria heading for Jerusalem, Luke records of Jesus that the Samaritans "did not receive Him, because His face was as though He would go to Jerusalem" (Luke 9:51–54). But James and John knew their Bibles! They knew that Elijah had called down fire from heaven onto people (2 Kings 1:10–12), so they said, "Lord, will Thou that we command fire to come down from heaven, and consume them, even as Elijah did?" (Luke 9:54). Of course, Jesus did not give permission.

This reinforces the principle that God is not bound by His past actions to duplicate them for our circumstances. We must not be presumptuous. He acts sovereignly to execute His plans. Because He healed one person does not mean that He must heal another.

The Sovereign Display of God's Mercy

Now let us examine Paul's three missionary journeys and his trip to Rome to face Caesar, and we will see how God used Paul to bring healing to suffering people. God brought these miracles to verify Paul's role as an apostle, but He did not always allow Paul to perform miracles at will.

We recommend that you keep your Bible open to follow these journeys. It would also be wise to refer to detailed maps in the back of your Bible or Bible atlas and trace these trips as we go.

• First Journey (Acts 13:4–14, 26)

Paul and Barnabas began their first journey by going to the island of Cyprus. "And when they were at Salamis, they preached the word of God in the synagogues of the Jews" (Acts 13:5). Notice that there were no healings recorded there, but the gospel was preached. Barnabas and Paul then proceeded to the western side of the island and came to Paphos where "they found a certain sorcerer, a false prophet, a Jew, whose name was Bar-jesus" (v. 6).

This Bar-jesus was also called Elymas and he resisted Barnabas and Paul's message to the island's governmental representative named Sergius Paulus (vv. 7–8). Because of this interference, Paul, "filled with the Holy Ghost, set his eyes on him" (v. 9) and declared temporary blindness upon him (v. 11).

Paul and Barnabas then traveled on to Pisidean Antioch and, as you recall from our look earlier at Galatians 4:13–14, Paul was sick. He had intended to go to Ephesus but circumstances prevented him. Antioch had an amphitheater that seated 24,500 people. We wonder if this was where Paul intended to preach. However, God hindered Paul at this time from going to Ephesus and diverted him to a different assignment.

When we examine Luke's account here at Antioch, we notice that no miracles were recorded. Not only could Paul not heal himself, but evidently he did not heal others either. Notice also that the fearless proclamation of the gospel resulted in severe persecution. Paul and Barnabas were "expelled . . . out of their coasts" (Acts 13:50). The word "expelled" is *ekbállō* (1544) and literally means to throw out. Paul was thrown out of Antioch!

Next, Paul and Barnabas proceeded to Iconium. "Long time therefore abode they speaking boldly in the Lord, which gave testimony unto the word of His grace, and granted signs and wonders to be done by their hands" (Acts 14:3). We are not specifically told what these signs and wonders were nor are we told how many were done. We do know though that it did not prevent persecution, for they were personally assaulted. Here these most wonderful "signs and wonders" were done, and still they were threatened with stoning! Again, they heard of the plot and "fled unto Lystra and Derbe" (Acts 14:6).

When they arrived in Lystra, Paul performed another miracle. "And there sat a certain man at Lystra, impotent in his feet, being a cripple from his mother's womb, who never had walked" (v. 8). At this particular juncture, Paul was permitted to heal this man: "and perceiving that he had faith to be healed, [he] said with a loud voice, Stand upright on thy feet. And he leaped and walked" (vv. 9–10). God enabled Paul to heal that total stranger, yet Paul could not heal his friends Epaphroditus (Phil. 2:25–27) nor Trophimus (2 Tim. 4:20), nor could he heal himself.

The reaction of the people of Lystra revealed the depth of their idolatry and superstition. They said, "The gods are come down to us in the likeness of men" (Acts 14:11). Then they wanted to offer sacrifices to Paul and Barnabas after they had reasoned that Barnabas was Jupiter and Paul was Mercury (vv. 12–13). Paul did not want any part of their adulation and said to them, "Sirs, why do you these things? We also are men of like passions with you" (v. 15). The phrase "men of like passions" is the same used to describe Elijah who also performed miracles (James 5:17).

You see, Paul and Barnabas would not take any credit for healing this lame man. It was not anything in *them* that restored his feet. They shifted the focus away from themselves to God who really did the healing when they said, "We also are men of like passions with you, and preach unto you that you should turn from these vanities unto the living God" (Acts 14:15). The people focused on the visible miracle, not the invisible miracle of the man's faith in Christ. The word "turn" here is *epistréphō* (1994) which is also used in James 5:19–20: "Brethren, if any of you do err from the truth, and one convert him; Let him know, that he which converts the sinner from the error of his way shall save a soul from death, and shall hide a multitude of sins." Paul seems to be echoing James' epistle as he speaks to the Lystrans.

But again, trouble-making Jews from Antioch and Iconium "persuaded the people, and, having stoned Paul, drew him out of the city, supposing he had been dead. Howbeit, as the disciples stood round about him, he rose up, and came into the city: and the next day he departed with Barnabas to Derbe" (Acts 14:19–20). God permitted Paul to perform the healing in Lystra for a purpose, and that was to impress the people that God's power was present.

Then Paul and Barnabas retraced their journey to the seaport of Perga and sailed to Syrian Antioch (Acts 14:21–28).

• Second Journey (Acts 15:11–18, 22)

From Syrian Antioch, Paul and Barnabas traveled to Jerusalem and met with the apostles and elders of the church. The inclusion of so many Gentiles into the church became the cause of some theological problems. The issue of circumcision was raised and discussed and rejected (Acts 15:5–21).

Paul, this time accompanied by Silas, began his second missionary journey (Acts 15:40–41). On this trip they delivered the letter authorized by the church council of Jerusalem (Acts 16:4). Paul then was given a vision to come over to Macedonia: "There stood a man of Macedonia, and prayed him, saying, Come over into Macedonia, and help us. And after he had seen the vision, immediately we endeavored to go into Macedonia, assuredly gathering that the Lord has called us to preach the gospel unto them" (Acts 16:9–10). Paul apparently wanted to stay in his native Asia Minor, but the Lord directed him otherwise. The phrase "assuredly gathering" is the word *sumbibázō* (4822) meaning to cause to come together. Paul considered the matter and was certain that it was God's will for him to go to Macedonia.

When he arrived in Philippi, Paul preached the gospel and Lydia was saved (Acts 16:14–15). He then performed a miracle of exorcism on a young girl with "a spirit of Python" which is the literal translation (Acts 16:16–18). This, of course, caused an uproar by her money-hungry owners, and Paul and Silas were beaten and jailed (Acts 16:20–24). These men followed the Lord's vision, and it led to their being beaten and thrown into jail. The purpose was soon to reveal itself, for their imprisonment was the means of the conversion of the Philippian jailer (Acts 16:30). So the occasional ability to cast out demons did not protect Paul from the harsh and cruel actions of others. However, the problems became opportunities in disguise.

Then Paul and Silas went on to Thessalonica for a three Sabbath Day stay, and not a single physical healing is recorded (Acts 17:1–9). But notice, the Lord did heal some people spiritually for in verse 4 we read, "And some of them believed." Then they went on to Berea, Athens, and Corinth (Acts 17:10—18:17), and there is not a single word indicating that Paul performed any miracles of healing in those cities. He spent an entire year and a half in Corinth with no recorded healings. Healing was certainly not a major emphasis of Paul's second journey.

• Third Journey (Acts 18:23—21:8)

On Paul's third missionary journey, he revisited the churches "of Galatia and Phrygia in order, strengthening all the disciples" (Acts 18:23). When he arrived in Ephesus, he taught in the Jewish synagogue (Acts 19:8), but a reaction and resistance set in. Nevertheless, verse 11 tells us that "God wrought special miracles by the hands of Paul." Now, why did God allow miracles in Ephesus but not in Corinth? We believe that the Lord granted these special miracles to validate Paul's ministry. Verse 12 reads, "So that from his body were brought unto the sick handkerchiefs or aprons, and the diseases departed from them, and the evil spirits went out of them."

Paul then traveled to Greece and stayed three months (Acts 20:2–3), retraced his steps back to Philippi, and sailed to Troas in Asia Minor (v. 6). At

Troas he preached "and continued his speech until midnight" (v. 7).

Now, observe what happened: "And there sat in a window a certain young man named Eutychus, being fallen into a deep sleep: and as Paul was long preaching, he sunk down with sleep, and fell down from the third loft, and was taken up dead" (v. 9). The name "Eutychus" means "man with good luck"—we might say, "Mr. Lucky." Well, this night he fell down and was thought to be dead, but in verse 10 it tells us that "Paul went down, and fell on him, and embracing him said, Trouble not yourselves; for his life is in him." Verse 12 completes the story: "And they brought the young man alive, and were not a little comforted."

Paul did not go to Troas to heal anyone. He did not advertise special healing services. On special occasions, the Lord allowed him to perform miracles.

Determined to go to Jerusalem, Paul met with the Ephesian church elders on the way. He warned them "that after my departing shall grievous wolves enter in among you, not sparing the flock" (v. 29). Then he mentions an internal threat: "Of your own selves shall men arise, speaking perverse things, to draw away disciples after them" (v. 30). Present day church leaders should heed this warning, too.

• Trip to Rome (Acts 27:1—28:15)

Paul was arrested in Jerusalem, appealed to Caesar, and was sent to Rome (Acts 27:1–12). On the way, a fierce storm caused a shipwreck (vv. 13–44). "And when they were escaped, then they knew that the island was called Melita" (Acts 28:1), which today we call Malta. God did not prevent the storm for Paul's sake, but He did protect him through it.

Once on shore, being cold and wet, a fire was lit. Then something unusual happened. "And when Paul had gathered a bundle of sticks, and laid them on the fire, there came a viper out of the heat and fastened on his hand" (v. 3). The native inhabitants, who knew that the snake was poisonous, assumed that Paul would soon die (v. 4), but Paul "shook off the beast into the fire, and felt no harm" (v. 5). So, instead of one dead apostle there was one dead snake! God here neutralized a snake bite, but Paul still had his "thorn in the flesh."

Publius, a courteous local government official, had a father who was "sick of a fever and of a bloody flux" (v. 8). The word for "bloody flux" is *dusentería* (1420) from which we get our medical term "dysentery." Webster defines it as "an infection of the lower intestinal tract producing pain, fever, and severe diarrhea, often with the passage of blood and mucus" (*Webster's II*, Houghton-Mifflin Co., Boston, 1994). Paul healed this man, and "when this was done, others also, which had diseases in the island, came, and were healed" (v. 9).

Have you noticed that as we have gone through the book of Acts that in the ministry of the apostle Paul there were only a few occasions for which miraculous healings were recorded although he ministered for thirty years? Without doubt, healing was not primary but incidental in his ministry. The preaching of the gospel was central for Paul. He himself wrote, "For I delivered unto you first of all that which I also received, how that Christ died for our sins" (1 Cor. 15:3). That was Paul's priority and focus, and we, too, would do well to keep first things first.

20

Paul's Teaching on Healing

As we have seen, the apostle Paul did perform certain healings during his thirty years of ministry, but they were not a frequent occurrence. We also saw that Paul did not consider healing to be his first priority nor did he ever claim to be a healer.

At this point we must ask, What did Paul actually teach concerning healing? When we examine the Pauline epistles, we find that he only wrote about healing in three verses! They are 1 Corinthians 12:9, 28, 30, and so the only church that Paul wrote to concerning healing was the Corinthian church.

When we look at the two epistles to Corinth we see a church torn with internal division, confusion on the key doctrine of the resurrection, a disruptive and shameful celebration of the Lord's Supper, generally disorderly worship services, immorality among the members, and Christians taking other Christians to court. This rather frightful picture looks very much like the church in our century. That is why it is important to see what Paul taught on this subject of healing as the needed correction to what we see in our churches today.

Healings Are the Result of God's Grace

In 1 Corinthians 12:9, the King James Version reads, "to another the gifts of healing." The word for "gifts" is *charísmata,* which is the plural of *chárisma* (5486). The root of both words is *cháris* (5485) which means "grace," and the suffix *–ma* at the end means the result of grace. You see, Paul is saying that what God gives to individuals is His grace.

In 1 Corinthians 1:7 Paul wrote "that you come behind in no gift." That is *chárisma.* Because the Corinthians had received the grace (*cháris*) of God, they had the potential of exhibiting any result of that grace, or *charísmata.*

We must remember that every Christian is indwelt by the Holy Spirit. We were all baptized in the Holy Spirit when we believed. That is what Paul wrote in 1 Corinthians 12:13: "For by one Spirit are we all baptized into one body, whether we be Jews or Gentiles, whether we be bond or free; and have been all made to drink into one Spirit." To not be baptized into the Holy Spirit is not to be saved at all. The work of the Holy Spirit in joining us to the body of Christ is a permanent work.

When God desires to exhibit or manifest His *cháris* (grace) through any of His children, He is able to give the *charísmata* (the results of grace) which is the result of the indwelling of the Spirit. It is not when you or I choose it to be, but rather when God chooses. He can heal our body or someone else's that we pray for, but we do not "own" the gift.

God can also give us grace to bear up under illness. The child of God takes illness as a gift from God to develop a closer relationship with Him. It takes a spirit-filled child of God to bear up sweetly and graciously through pain and suffering rather than constantly whining and crying for healing. We should pray by all means, but pray for His will to be done.

Even as we saw in Paul's case, the gift of healing was not inherent with him. It was a temporary, supernatural enablement that came relatively infrequently to him. Since it was not permanent with even the apostle Paul, we must not regard the various gifts of God as our particular, permanent possession. It is the enablement of the Holy Spirit that the *cháris* (grace) expresses itself in the *chárisma* (the result of grace), whether it is in healing or in the performing of some miracle that is outside of the ordinary.

Healings Are One among Many of the Gifts

As we noted earlier, 1 Corinthians 12 is the only place where Paul dealt with the gifts of healings (vv. 9, 28, 30). He speaks of this gift, not in isolation but in the larger context of all the gifts which God gives.

In verse 7, Paul says, "But the manifestation of the Spirit is given to every man." God chooses individuals, not groups, to endow with His grace, and, furthermore, He chooses individuals whom He allows to demonstrate different evidences of His grace.

Later on in verses 12 to 27, Paul uses the superb example that one body has different members. We have fingers—in fact, ten fingers—but they are all different. We have ears, a mouth, a tongue, and so on. And God made us, the members of His body, different, not carbon copies, and He gives different gifts to different people.

None of the gifts Paul lists is an inherent grace. No one should ever feel that he has a gift that he can use any way and any time he wants. The only one who ever had inherent power or authority in heaven and on earth was Jesus Christ (Matt. 28:18), and He allows individuals to be used by Him as He so chooses. Paul said, "But all these work that one and the selfsame Spirit, dividing to every man severally as He will" (1 Cor. 12:11). Notice that it is up to God, not up to us.

Not only is the Lord the One in charge, He is the focus of the work, not us. How quick we are to forget this! And much of the time we do not have the attitude that John the Baptist had when he said, "He must increase, but I must decrease" (John 3:30). Even the Holy Spirit who gives these gifts does not focus on Himself. He points to Jesus. "But when the Comforter is come, whom I will send unto you from the Father, even the Spirit of truth, which proceeds from the Father, He shall testify of Me" (John 15:26). Jesus told us plainly what our attitude should be: "So likewise you, when you shall have done all those things which are commanded you, say, We are unprofitable servants: we have done that which was our duty to do" (Luke 17:10).

Paul states that these gifts are for the benefit of the entire body, not just one person's benefit. He said, "to profit withal" (1 Cor. 12:7). The word is *sumphérō* (4851). He used it earlier in 1 Corinthians 6:12 where it is translated "expedient" which means profitable or beneficial. These gifts are given to individuals; not so that they may profit financially or egotistically, but to build up all the Christians in the fellowship.

Then Paul goes on to list these various gifts in verses 8 to 10. One is given "the word of wisdom" (v. 8). This is the ability, the intelligence, to be wise. The word "wisdom" is *sophía* (4678). It is the ability to understand our relationship to God.

In the same verse, Paul then says, "to another the word of knowledge." The word "another" is *állos* (243), meaning of the same kind or quality. God the Spirit gives different gifts, but they all have their place, and one person's gift is no better or worse, greater or smaller, since they are all necessary for everyone's growth. What is this "word of knowledge"? It is what can be learned from the study of what God has given.

In verse 9 Paul says, "to another faith by the same Spirit." This is the God-given faith to accomplish certain things He wants that individual to do. It is faith beyond ordinary faith, perhaps to face a difficult personal crisis or to witness more effectively. Perhaps Stephen had this special, powerful faith because we read, "And Stephen, full of faith and power, did great wonders and miracles among the people" (Acts 6:8), and at the close of his testimony, Luke wrote that Stephen was "full of the Holy Ghost" (Acts 7:55).

Paul then names the "gifts of healing" in 1 Corinthians 12:9. It should be properly translated as two plurals: "gifts of healings." This is the result of God's grace which actually precedes the healing. That *–ma* at the end of *chárisma* is emphasizing that it is the grace of God in us which is supernaturally given us through the operation of the Holy Spirit. The word "healings" is *íama* (2386) (note the *–ma* suffix; plural genitive *iamátōn*) or that which is the result of healing, not the actual healing process (*íasis* [2392]).

The reason it is in the plural form is that there are various and diverse kinds of healings. There is no one method of healing. We certainly remember that our Lord Jesus used many different methods when He healed (touch, the spoken word, etc.). Paul is saying that the Lord chooses one individual to give healing to another. Yet, in this world, they are all still temporary. We may be healed by the Lord, but unless His return is during our lifetime, we will surely die.

Have you noticed how often in 1 Corinthians 12 the apostle Paul uses the phrase "by the same Spirit"? There should be no superiority and no room for boasting by anyone whom God uses.

Continuing with the gifts, Paul says, "To another the working of miracles" (v. 10). There is nothing here that speaks of an inherent ability in man. It is always the supernatural manifestation of the Spirit of God as He is pleased to show Himself. How well Paul knew this! Paul was nothing but God's vessel into which His grace was poured. Ananias was told by the Lord that Paul "is a chosen vessel unto Me" (Acts 9:15). Paul himself said, "If a man therefore purge himself from these, he shall be a vessel unto honor, sanctified, and meet for the Master's use" (2 Tim. 2:21). A vessel is nothing but a container to be used. In and of itself it is nothing significant.

Continuing in 1 Corinthians 12:10, Paul wrote, "to another prophecy, to another discerning of spirits." Here are gifts which the pastors of a church would need. The word "prophecy" is *prophēteía* (4394). This is proclaiming God's grace to others. It is "forth-telling" the good news! It is not the office, but the function Paul speaks of here. The word "discerning" is *diákrisis* (1253) and means to separate one from another. How important that this gift be used in the church at Corinth! How important for the church today! We need our shepherds to discern the wolves around and among the flock.

Then, "to another diverse kinds of tongues." Here the word "another" is *héteros* (2087) which means another of a different kind. We are not all alike, nor are we supposed to be. These "tongues" are not the same as Pentecost's events but are the ability to learn certain families of languages. Those who say that all should speak in ecstatic tongues are wrong on both counts—neither *all* nor *ecstatic languages* are meant.

In all these instances of the phrase "gifts of healings" (vv. 9, 28, 30), the emphasis is that it is the Lord who determines how His grace is distributed. That is why it is called a "gift" (1 Cor. 1:7); it is a "grace," and grace, by its very definition, cannot be and is not something earned nor forced from the Lord's hand.

Healings Are for God's Ultimate Purpose

God had a purpose in demonstrating His miracles of healing throughout the Old Testament and the New Testament. They proved that God was mightier than man and his problems. They also pointed to the saving, rescuing power of God. God is a God who reaches out to fallen man.

Now, you must remember that it is the same God who lives today that lived in the age of the patriarchs, the prophets, and the apostles. In His essence and nature He does not, cannot, change. In how He works, though, He does change.

We have that specifically stated in Hebrews 1:1, 2: "God, who at sundry times and diverse manners spoke in time past unto the fathers by the prophets, has in these last days spoken unto us by His Son." Since God has spoken clearly by His Son, we have no excuse. Like a good parent, the Lord explained things gradually to His creation, and He did that in a variety of ways. God's methods of dealing with His children have changed. We cannot assume that what He did for Moses or Elijah or Paul, He is obligated to do for us.

As we have shown earlier, until our bodies are glorified (see 1 Cor. 15:52ff.), we will be subject to sickness and death. Though we have the first fruits of the Spirit that bring to life our dead spirits, we must not assume that our bodies have changed, too. We are not "supermen," immune from death. Rather, we eagerly await our changed bodies at the resurrection.

Can God heal as He did before? Of course He can. Remember, the whole healing ability is called *chárisma,* a gift of God. We do not go to our heavenly Father making a demand anymore than we would go to our earthly father and demand some benefit from him. We pray, "Thy will be done."

In the middle of this discussion of various gifts, Paul says, "God has tempered the body together . . . that there should be no schism in the body; but that the members should have the same care one for another" (1 Cor. 12:24–25). We must remember above everything else that the gifts God gives us are given for the benefit of all in the body. They are not given to promote our pride or our power, but to serve the Body of Christ more effectively.

Also notice that nowhere does Paul say that God has placed "healers" in the church. No, He has placed "gifts of healings" (1 Cor. 12:9). Paul says in verse 28 that God has given "first apostles, secondarily prophets." He was to later write to the Ephesians that the household of God was "built upon the foundation of apostles and prophets," and that "foundation period" was completed in the first century. Consequently, the offices of apostle and prophet do not exist today. Today there are no apostles. If there were, then what they wrote would be Scripture.

We, as believers, have the right to pray for God's healing for ourselves and others. At times, God will answer that prayer affirmatively if it is in His plan and purpose. He can use you to display His grace.

Healings Are According to God's Timetable

Paul was the same apostle who wrote 1 Corinthians, Romans, and Ephesians. In these three epistles he mentions the gifts of the Spirit, but it is only in the Corinthian epistles that the gifts of healings are mentioned.

As we look at the overall picture of healings and miracles in the Bible, we notice that there are actually only a few miracles spread out over a thousand years in the Old Testament. When we reach the life of Jesus, we find a much greater number compressed into a little over three years. In the apostolic age, we see the number diminishing.

For instance, the apostle Paul wrote to the Corinthians about the gifts of healings. 1 Corinthians was written around A.D. 59, but when we come to Romans 12, we do not find any mention of the gifts of healings. In the list given in verses 6 to 8, various gifts are mentioned. Did the gifts of healings stop? They were, at least, less important or not noteworthy. The epistle of Romans is dated at A.D. 60, one year after the Corinthian epistle.

Why were there so many healings during the ministry years of the Lord Jesus Christ? Why this surge of miracle working? The apostle Peter gives us the answer in Acts 2:22: "You men of Israel, hear these words; Jesus of Nazareth, a man approved of God among you by miracles and wonders and signs." What was the reason? It was to prove the deity of Jesus Christ. To repeat them now is not necessary. He displayed an abundance of miracles because He was the only One who has the power inherently in Himself. Jesus has already proven who He is and that He has all power in heaven and on earth (Matt. 28:18), and He has warned that it is a wicked and adulterous generation that seeks after signs (Matt. 12:39).

Then we come to the epistle to the Ephesians. This was written in A.D. 64, five years later than 1 Corinthians. In Ephesians 4:11 Paul wrote, "And He gave some, apostles; and some, prophets; and some, evangelists; and some, pastors and teachers."

We noted before that the offices of apostle and prophet were foundational (Eph. 2:20). What we have today are evangelists and pastors and teachers. There is no office of "healer" mentioned. There is no mention in Ephesians of the gifts of healings.

We must ask ourselves who is getting the glory when we minister? Is it we ourselves, or do we keep the focus on the Lord Jesus Christ? Do we not see how man-centered the church has become? Are we not too much like Corinth and not enough like Philippi? We must keep before us Isaiah 42:8, "I am the Lord: that is My name: and My glory will I not give to another."

Scripture Index